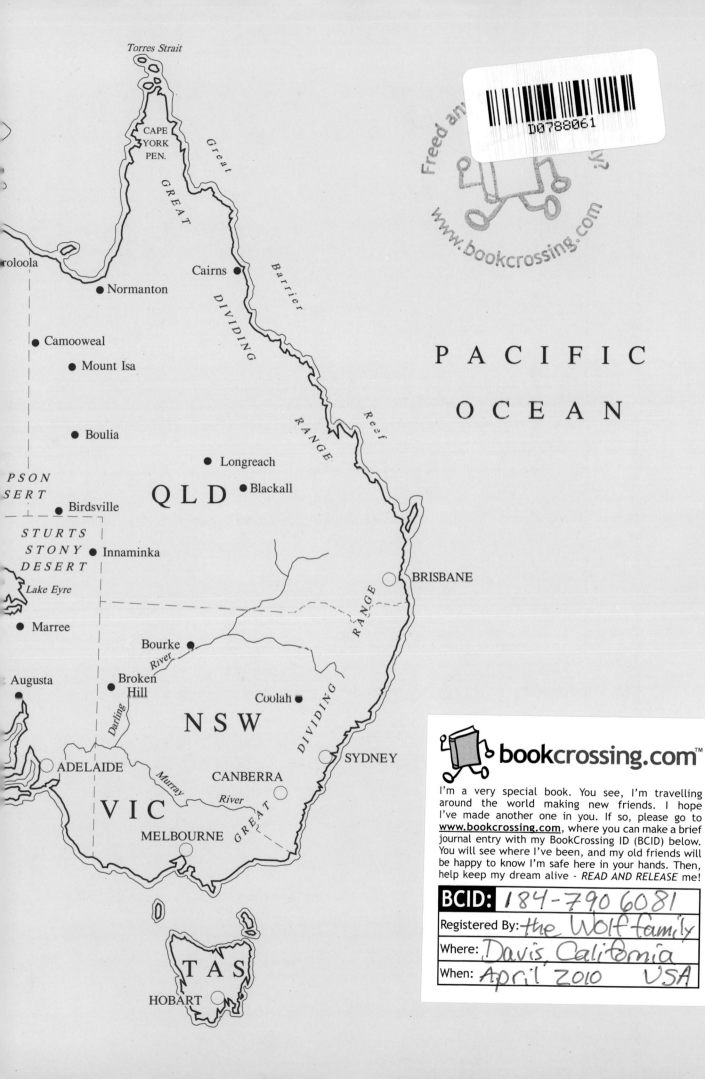

Torres Strait

CAPE
YORK
PEN.

Great

G R E A T

roloola

Cairns

Barrier

Normanton

D I V I D I N G

Camooweal

Mount Isa

PACIFIC

OCEAN

Boulia

Reef

Longreach

R A N G E

QLD

Blackall

PSON
SERT

Birdsville

STURTS
STONY
DESERT

Innaminka

Lake Eyre

BRISBANE

Marree

RANGE

Bourke

River

Augusta

Broken
Hill

Coolah

Darling

NSW

DIVIDING

Adelaide

SYDNEY

Murray

CANBERRA

River

VIC

GREAT

MELBOURNE

TAS

HOBART

Australia's
OUTBACK

Twin Ghost Gums, near Alice Springs

Australia's OUTBACK

JOURNEYS AND DISCOVERIES

JOCELYN BURT

HOUGHTON MIFFLIN COMPANY
Boston New York London
1992

I would like to thank the following for their assistance with this book: Russell Guest 4x4 Safaris, Melbourne; Dick Lang of Desert-Trek Australia, Adelaide; Ian and Sue Sinnamon, Home Valley Station, east Kimberley; Jack and Neroli Roberts, Kununurra; Slingsby Helicopters, Kununurra; Horst and Evelin Faustmann, Darwin; Lloyd and Audrey Cutler, Cooinda; Conservation Commission of the Northern Territory; Department of Conservation and Land Management, Western Australia; National Parks and Wildlife Service, South Australia; National Parks and Wildlife Service, Queensland; National Parks and Wildlife Service, New South Wales; Australian National Parks and Wildlife Service.

Nearly all the photographs for this book were taken on Fuji RDP film, and most of the photographs were taken with a Mamiya RB67 camera.

FOR MY MOTHER

First published 1992 by
Jacaranda Wiley
33 Park Road, Milton, Qld 4064
Offices also in Sydney, Melbourne and Auckland

This edition published 1992 by
Houghton Mifflin Company
2 Park Street, Boston, Massachusetts 02108

© Jocelyn Burt

CIP data is available.
ISBN 0-395-66014-9

Printed in Hong Kong

CONTENTS

Dune, South Australia

PREFACE

Many people will tell you that Australia's soul lies somewhere in the ancient-looking and worn land of the continent's outback. Where its spirit may be exactly doesn't matter, for everyone will find it in a different place. For some it may lie deep in a craggy, colourful gorge, or in a strange monolith flaring red at sunrise or sunset, or by a river of sand lined with big red gums. For others, it may be a lily-covered billabong where herons, egrets and honking hordes of magpie geese feed, and where restless, screeching corellas festoon nearby trees like cottonwool. Or it may be in the immense desert plains with their red sand-dunes, white salt pans, seas of shimmering gibber stones, and far horizons that stretch the mind and evoke a tremendous sense of awe.

There is no specific boundary to the outback; some even say it begins and ends in our minds. Broadly, it applies to the land lying beyond the coastal cities, towns, the settled rural areas, and the green slopes of the Great Dividing Range; this means that it covers more than three-quarters of the continent.

A good portion of the outback pushes into tropical regions, where the climate is more stable with its two distinct seasons, the Wet and the Dry. Despite the lush tropical vegetation around its rivers and lagoons, this northern region is as inhospitable, and as sparsely populated, as the rest of the outback. Further inland, the climate can be unpredictable, since normal weather-patterns are frequently disrupted by droughts or excessive rains.

The outback may be harsh, but there is little doubt that its 1 500 000 square kilometres contain some of the Earth's most unusual scenery. Its warm, rich colours are a delight for photographers and artists. No scene is the same in the morning as in the afternoon, at sunrise as at sunset, for the land responds wonderfully to the changes of light as the sun progresses across the sky. The outback has a character and atmosphere that is as unique as its scenery. It is often full of surprises: who would think that one of the country's toughest mining towns would have more art galleries than pubs? Broken Hill, in New South Wales, is home to some of Australia's most famous outback artists.

For the Aborigines, the original inhabitants, much of the outback is a ritual ground of sacred Dreamtime legends. For white Australians, it is the heartland of our legends and traditions: since its settlement, seemingly ordinary men and women have carried out many extraordinary feats, often under severe hardship, in a land that will never tolerate the weak. These remarkable people and their exploits now live on in the outstanding Stockman's Hall of Fame, in Longreach, western Queensland.

For many visitors, there is often a heightened expectation of adventure when setting out for a journey to the outback. This is largely because much of the region is still 'last frontier' country. It should never be taken lightly by travellers, however experienced. Adequate preparation is essential, and even if visitors only hire a car to drive from one outback town to another, it is imperative they carry extra drinking water should a breakdown occur. For most of my trips made over many years, I travelled in an assortment of Hiace two-wheel-drive (2WD) campervans. At times it was necessary to take commercial tours to areas that were unsuitable for the vans. Just before preparing this book I changed to a four-wheel-drive (4WD) Landcruiser campervan.

In this book, through the photographs and by recounting some of my journeys and discoveries, I hope to give the reader — and the prospective traveller — an insight to Australia's outback. For those who have already been, I hope many pleasant memories will be refreshed, and a better understanding gained of a region that I firmly believe to be one of the most exciting in the world.

Finke River, Glen Helen

The Amphitheatre, near Palm Valley

Standley Chasm

THE RED CENTRE

X

THE RED CENTRE

The DC3 aircraft touched down at Alice Springs. A bus looking as if it had been requisitioned from the wrecker's yard waited outside the terminal to take our small group to one of three hotels in town, the Mount Gillen Chalet. Lying near the railway line at the edge of the town and constructed largely from galvanised-iron, the chalet nestled in bushland backed by a colourful rugged range. Long sheds divided into small rooms served as sleeping quarters for the guests. In mine, at one end, sunlight streamed through a myriad of tiny holes that pricked the iron walls and ceilings, giving the room a star-spangled look. I wondered what would happen if it rained; judging by the drought-stricken, dusty reddish landscapes around the town, that was unlikely to happen.

The few tourists in the town were mostly old women and interstate school children; I was with a school group. We laughed at the standard of accommodation, at every rough and ready meal that had the same lavish garnish of tinned diced mixed vegetables, but we lapped up the character of the place, with its warm and friendly atmosphere. The town was like no other we had seen, and every second shop seemed to be either a milk bar or stockmen's outfitters selling everything from soap to boomerangs. Everybody was so friendly.

We visited some gorges in the nearby MacDonnell Ranges, including dramatic Standley Chasm, a narrow 60-metre-high gash best seen at midday when the walls briefly flamed rich shades of gold and red. Nobody else was around; indeed, we had all the gorges to ourselves. We travelled everywhere in ancient buses — 'old bombs' we called them, because no trip was made without a breakdown of some sort occurring — that meant sometimes waiting hours on the side of the road for a replacement. This wasn't surprising, considering the fast speed the drivers took the buses over the appallingly rough tracks that served as roads. By the time we reached Palm Valley, after negotiating a track that followed the bed of the Finke River for sixteen kilometres, twisting through deep, loose sand and over rocks and bushes, it was a miracle the bus, and its passengers, were still in one piece.

At Palm Valley, a tent city spread beside the Amphitheatre, a splendid semicircular range eroded into bold spires, high headlands and sheer slopes. Near the tents stood a large galvanised-iron shed serving as a dining room that we shared with other school groups. The hot sunny days were spent climbing Battleship and Initiation Rocks in the Amphitheatre, and exploring Palm Valley, with its ancient cycads and *Livistona* palms — remnants of a past era when tropical vegetation covered central Australia.

Every night we sat around a blazing camp fire and listened to our guide tell exciting stories about the region. Later, when everyone was in bed, we crept out of our tents and by the light of the full moon stumbled up a nearby rocky hill. Once at the top, we sat for a long time, absorbing the atmosphere; now and then the deep silence of the night was broken by a mournful howl of a dingo, its eerie call sending shivers down our spines. It was marvellous.

That was central Australia in 1957. By the 1990s Alice Springs had metamorphosed into a very large modern town, with a bewildering number of hotels, motels, cabins, camping grounds, car rental firms, shops, supermarkets, restaurants, art galleries and other tourist attractions. Every day fleets of air-conditioned luxury coaches carry tourists in comfort along sealed or good gravel roads to the many scenic attractions, which can be very crowded during the winter peak holiday season. As for Palm Valley, the tent city has long gone, and the place is part of the Finke Gorge National Park. Although access is still limited to 4WD vehicles because of the rocks and sand, so much work has been done to the track running up the Finke River (there is even a small patch of bitumen) that it is an easy drive to the camping ground. As for climbing the rocky hills at night without a torch: no way would I attempt that now because of the chance of stepping on a death adder.

The heart of the outback, central Australia is affectionately known as 'The Red Centre', because the colour red dominates so many scenes — particularly at sunrise and sunset.

Palm Valley

Lying almost in the dead centre of the continent, with the cities of Darwin 1534 kilometres to the north and Adelaide 1687 kilometres to the south, Alice Springs is the unofficial capital of the region. The nearest town is Tennant Creek, 507 kilometres away. Many visitors fly to Alice Springs, though probably many more come by coach and in their own vehicles, travelling via the Stuart Highway, now a wide bitumen road that runs from Port Augusta to Darwin. A number of petrol stations dot the highway to serve travellers; all have motel rooms, camping ground and a cafe.

Some of the best scenery in the entire outback lies in the rocky and colourful MacDonnell Ranges that flank Alice Springs for many kilometres to the east and west. Spectacular gorges, gaps and chasms slash its craggy folds; one of them, Heavitree Gap, lies in Alice Springs, and through it squeezes a road, railway line and the Todd River; occasionally the river of sand becomes a raging torrent of water and fills the entire gap.

MacDonnell Ranges, near Glen Helen

THE RED CENTRE

Paper daisies, eastern MacDonnell Ranges

Trephina Gorge

THE RED CENTRE

Ruby Gorge

Perentie

In general, the eastern MacDonnells are not as grand as the western section; however, Trephina Gorge, lying 76 kilometres out from Alice Springs, is a 'must' for visitors. The approach to Trephina is a scenic treat, as great bastions of red rock guard Trephina Creek at the entrance to the gorge. Inside the gorge, the beauty of its rugged red walls is enhanced by white-limbed ghost gums growing among the rocks and a permanent pool of water that on still days mirrors everything. For many years during the 1970s there was no pool, as an exceptionally heavy flood swept it away. Without it, the gorge lost much of its character, but all that was needed was another big flood to gouge out a depression in the sand to enable a pool to remain once the flood waters had subsided.

Just outside the gorge stands a large ghost gum that is probably the finest to be seen anywhere. I first photographed it with a Box Brownie in 1957. The last time I saw it — over thirty years later — it still looked as if it had been whitewashed before dawn, its blemish-free bark appearing to fit the tree like a glove, wrinkling at the fork of the limbs in the manner of a soft fabric. Touch its bark, and a fine white dust covers your hand. These pristine white trees, called ghost gums because on moonlit nights their gleaming white trunks give a ghostly quality to the landscape, are a dominant feature of the Mac-Donnell Ranges.

Galahs, Stuart Highway

A 4WD vehicle is needed for exploring much of the country beyond Trephina Gorge, particularly if visiting Ruby Gorge in the Atnarpa Range. The track to the gorge — and the gorge itself — at times has some treacherous quicksand, and it is not unknown for stock to be swallowed by the quicksands here; a heavy vehicle would have little chance. I first heard about it from an Alice Springs local who declared it to be a 'top spot'; he also warned about the quicksand. Armed with this information, I managed to persuade a group of friends to go there. We reached the gorge safely, though if there had been much more moisture around we would have run into serious trouble at several creek crossings, which were very soft. The only real quicksand was in the gorge itself.

My first impression of this large gorge was one of spaciousness. Both sides were lined with towering spinifex-covered slopes topped by great jagged collars of rock that dwarfed all vegetation. A long shallow pool of water lay about a kilometre up the gorge. But it was not easy walking to reach the pool: often what looked like a firm piece of ground turned out to be sand so soft that my leg disappeared up to the knee.

If a visitor has only time for one day of sightseeing, I would suggest a trip through the western MacDonnell Ranges to Glen Helen, 134 kilometres from Alice Springs, and, on the way, visit all the gorges: Simpsons and Honeymoon Gaps, Standley Chasm, Ellery, Serpentine and Ormiston Gorges. Better still, a night should be spent at Glen Helen to see its massive red cliffs at sunrise or sunset reflecting in a pool of the Finke River. From here there are superb views of Mount Sonder, particularly at dawn when it becomes a poem of mauves and pinks as the first rays of the sun light its distinct shape.

If you are out early in the morning at Glen Helen — always the best time in the outback — you may hear the hauntingly beautiful notes of butcherbirds, the chattering of grey-crowned babblers, and the screeches of cockatoos and brilliantly coloured galahs. These sounds, and the wonderful scenery along the Finke River, epitomise the unique character of central Australia. I am often asked which is my favourite place in Australia: there are many, but the country around Glen Helen is high on my list.

The largest and most interesting gorge lying between Alice Springs and Glen Helen is Ormiston Gorge, which is part of the Ormiston Gorge and Pound National Park. Situated twelve kilometres from Glen Helen, access is via a good bitumen road that goes to the information centre, camping ground and carpark; from here it is a five minute walk to the permanent pool in the gorge. To appreciate the full grandeur of Ormiston and its high colourful walls, it is best to walk right through the gorge, which takes about an hour. Many people are deterred by the barrier of rocks on the right, near the end of the main pool. However, if you find them too daunting, it is easy enough to go around by wading through the water — providing the pool is not full. Once at the end, the gorge opens out into Ormiston Pound, and a marked trail continues for nearly six kilometres through the pound and over the hills back to the carpark.

The ranger advised me to do this walk starting from the pound end, instead of in the gorge. 'In the morning the sun will be behind you, and the high walls around the gorge entrance will be lit — in the afternoon they are in shadow,' he said. I followed his advice, and discovered that by approaching the gorge this way the scenery was far better than if I had walked out of the gorge and then crossed the pound — as most people do. I also suspected it was easier to follow the yellow markers this way.

Ormiston Gorge

Paddy-melons

It is not possible to walk through all the gorges in the MacDonnell Ranges. Some have pools that brim to both sides of sheer walls, and the only way to explore them is by swimming or floating through on a rubber li-lo. However, it is more sensible to do this in the warmer months and not mid winter when the water is ice-cold — as I once discovered at Redbank Gorge. This gorge lies 21 kilometres beyond Glen Helen; the last four kilometres are extremely rough and 2WD vehicles need to take it with extreme care. From the carpark it is a twenty-minute walk to the entrance of this very narrow gorge where a series of pools lie within its precipitous walls.

My 'vessel' for exploring the gorge was a li-lo, on which I hoped to stay reasonably dry; however, I hadn't bargained on half rolling off it during the initial launch into the freezing water of the shaded first pool. Each pool was separated by a rocky section so slippery under wet feet that I ran more risk of breaking an ankle than catching pneumonia from the cold. I wondered if it would be warmer in summer as little, if any sunlight would penetrate this gorge. The exceptionally craggy walls, beautifully tinted in reds, browns, pinks, mauves and whites, tended to close in above, restricting the available light. In one place the gorge widened only at water-level, giving the effect of a cave; an eerie stillness pervaded the dimly lit scene, and the walls were so perfectly reflected in the pool that I felt as if I were floating on a mirror.

While in Redbank Gorge the words of a local rang constantly through my mind: 'Watch out for the big python that lives there. You'll see him on a ledge above one of the pools.' After negotiating about five or six pools, I came to a section so narrow I couldn't get the li-lo through and so I turned back. Thankfully, the python was nowhere in sight; I wasn't in the mood for meeting several metres of snake. Later someone informed me that it lived by the twelfth pool. However, I didn't mind photographing a perentie back at the carpark; the perentie is Australia's largest goanna and grows up to 2.5 metres long.

There is one other place lying beyond Glen Helen that is of great interest: Gosses Bluff. Situated about 200 kilometres from Alice Springs, Gosses Bluff resembles a gigantic pound or amphitheatre, its imposing walls towering to nearly 200 metres over the plains, falling away only in one small spot to allow entry. The track into the four-kilometre-wide valley is rough and broken in places by washaways, so a 4WD vehicle is recommended. As Gosses Bluff has been handed back to the Aboriginal traditional owners, it is now necessary to get a permit from the Central Land Council in Alice Springs to travel the road into the place, and camping is no longer permitted.

There has been much speculation about how Gosses Bluff was formed. Some scientists believe it to be the result of complex geological pressures that occurred millions of years ago, but others say it could be a meteorite crater. If it is the latter, Gosses Bluff would be one of the largest craters on the Earth's surface. Whatever its origins may be it is a beautiful place, and from the air it is an amazing sight. When I visited it, the valley was a mass of wildflowers as there had been record-breaking winter rains throughout the Centre. Everywhere that year the flowers were unbelievable, lining roads and covering sand-dunes like massed gardens. Even the paddy-melons proliferated into vast carpets, with some growing as big as commercially grown melons.

The wild paddy-melons intrigue many travellers because the sight of a mass of juicy-looking melons scrambling over the arid ground is at odds with the native vegetation. Although a trouble-some weed, in times of drought they are split open for the cattle to eat — despite the popular theory that stock may go blind. It is highly unlikely that people would suffer blindness if they ate one: the taste is so vile and bitter that after one mouthful it would be hastily thrown away.

Mount Sonder at sunrise

Mount Sonder and the Finke River

THE RED CENTRE

13

Gosses Bluff

Sand-dune

Most visitors find Alice Springs an excellent base to explore the surrounding country, while others prefer to use the bush camps located in some of the parks in the MacDonnell Ranges. However, many people will be drawn from their bush camps and even from other areas of the country into Alice Springs to see such hilarious annual events as the Henley-on-Todd regatta and the Camel Cup. The Henley-on-Todd is held in the wide and dry sandy creek bed of the Todd River, with the 'boats' powered only by human legs or by participants laboriously shovelling sand. The finale is the great 'sea battle' in which the ships are powerful 4WD vehicles suitably dressed as floats that bristle with imaginative ammunition and manned by crews of tough Territorians. The winner is the 'ship' last bogged in the sand — or the last to run out of ammunition.

The year I watched the sea battle, the ammunition was water hose guns, smoke and flour bombs, and an assortment of missiles ranging from rotten fruit and vegetables to banging crackers. I was able to seek asylum on the media stand; however, when we were enveloped in thick purple smoke from a badly-aimed bomb it didn't seem much of a refuge after all. 'It gets wilder every year,' muttered another photographer as we tried to cover our cameras. It was indeed wild, and the crowd loved every minute of it. I suspect this thoroughly Territorian event could only occur in the Northern Territory.

The Camel Cup is almost as funny though probably provides more frustration for the spectators. At the start of the race the camels may refuse to get up; then, if they decide to heed the frantic pleas of the jockeys — and those of the equally frantic punters — the animals may race off in a direction totally different from that of the set track. Many of the camels in the race come from the various camel farms where tourists can take a ride lasting from a few minutes to many days. My one and only ride on a camel at a farm in Alice Springs took place a few weeks before the Camel Cup, and all the beasts were in training for the race. Instead of taking a leisurely ride around the paddock, our three camels, each carrying two passengers, were lined up and without warning all were given a verbal command combined with a whack on the back that sent them into a fast gallop. The one I was riding somehow managed to escape from the paddock and we ended up out on the road, clinging precariously to the saddle.

Probably the greatest drawcard to central Australia is Uluru National Park, the home of Ayers Rock and the Olgas, two of the world's most outstanding natural wonders. Ayers Rock is the largest piece of exposed rock in the world, and the Olgas are a collection of fantastic domes set in a circle just to the west. Although the Rock is geologically distinct from the Olgas, both formations are sandstone and each is the revealed surface of a huge parent rock buried in the sandy plain. Both places are sacred symbols of the Aboriginal Dreamtime legends.

Lying about 450 kilometres south-west of Alice Springs, access to Uluru is by a good bitumen road. Just outside the park is Yulara, built for the express purpose of providing facilities for the growing number of tourists who come here. Since Yulara was established and the park was handed back to the Aboriginal traditional owners in the mid 1980s, many changes have occurred and, at the request of the Aborigines, quite a few places have been closed off to the public. When the re-routed bitumen road was completed to the Olgas in 1990, the old road — including the ring road around the Olgas — was closed, and so was the walk to the top of the dome Katajuta from where you could see one of Australia's greatest panoramas. Visitors can only explore Mount Olga Gorge, and the Valley of the Winds via a new walking access opened on the western side. Although tourists may photograph freely in the park, professional photographers and artists are now severely restricted in what they may portray.

Sea battle, Henley-on-Todd

Boat race, Henley-on-Todd

Camel-riding

Climbing the 348-metre-high Ayers Rock is still permitted and continues to be a popular thing to do, in spite of the fact it is difficult and, if you stray from the white line, dangerous. Everyone seems to want to attempt it, despite age, level of fitness, or suitability of dress. Over the years since my first visit to the park in 1974 I have seen some strange sights on the climb: women in tight skirts, high heels and carrying shopping bags, while others wore thongs, neck braces and blankets. Most people walk the steep area by the chain far too quickly, and it is not uncommon to see gasping elderly tourists looking as if they are about to have a stroke when they stop to catch their breath. One 89-year-old man managed to reach the top and return. Most people take a good hour to go up, and return in about half the time.

Another highlight is to see the Rock at sunset. Every evening the area known as Sunset Strip is packed with cars and coaches, and hundreds of people take up positions on the plain, waiting for that magical moment when it briefly flares red just before the sun dips below the horizon. There is also a sunset viewing area at the Olgas. Personally, I find the Olgas more stunning at sunset than the Rock.

Lying between Uluru National Park and Alice Springs is another remarkable place: Kings Canyon, in Watarrka National Park. Visitors travelling to Uluru often include a visit to Kings Canyon, as it is only 170 kilometres from the Yulara road. Part of the George Gill Range and with immense walls that look as if they have been sliced by a colossal knife, this incredible canyon is bordered by a plateau comprising a maze of small valleys topped by domed ridges of rock with a texture so old-looking that the overall effect is one of a ruined city. Down in the canyon, 180 metres below, lie enormous boulders that broke away from the north wall many years ago; some cracked sections of the south wall give the impression that it will not be too long before they join the breakaway boulders below. The views from the head of the canyon are breathtaking.

Kings Canyon also has undergone some changes in recent years. On a recent visit I was saddened to see that the bush camping ground by the carpark at the start of the canyon walk had been closed; the closest accommodation is now ten kilometres away at the Wilderness Lodge (which has a camping ground). However, I was delighted — and very relieved — to find that the clifftop canyon walk had been made considerably safer than it used to be; it has also been extended along the south wall, opening up more stunning vistas of the canyon and other parts of the George Gill Range. It had been eleven years since my last visit. Then there were no markers at all along the route, and it was estimated that 75 per cent of the walkers not on guided tours missed reaching the head of the canyon. If you wanted to explore the beautiful Garden of Eden, a narrow cleft full of lush vegetation tucked behind the head of the canyon, you risked life and limb getting into the place — that is, if you could find the way down. Today, the entire walk is well marked, and staircases have been built to provide safe access in and out.

I think the six-kilometre canyon walk is one of the best in central Australia. It takes three to four hours, starting with a steep climb to the plateau, then generally follows the canyon rim before descending to the carpark. As some people have died on this walk (mostly from heart attacks and heat exhaustion in the summer months), a notice at the carpark warns it is not for the unfit or disabled. There is easier walking in Kings Creek near the canyon's entrance.

Ayers Rock

The Olgas

THE RED CENTRE

A chapter on the 'Red Centre' would not be complete without mentioning the Devil's Marbles, a fascinating collection of boulders that lie scattered for many hectares just off the Stuart Highway, 400 kilometres north of Alice Springs. They come in a variety of shapes and sizes, some standing alone, others piled on top of each other. All show some degree of roundness, or of softening at the edges, and some are almost spherical, resembling monstrous cannonballs as they balance precariously on larger boulders or nestle in beds of corn-coloured grass. Aboriginal legend has it that the Marbles are the eggs of the Rainbow Serpent, a Dreamtime being linked with the source of all life. Geologists say that these stones were formed over the years by the elements.

The old Stuart Highway used to meander through the Marbles — and this road now forms the detour for motorists to see them. A small bush camping ground behind a large cluster of bun-like boulders provides a welcome break for travellers on their way to the tropical top of the Northern Territory. Now that the highway lies further away it is a much quieter place to spend a night — the road trains are only a distant roar.

Kings Creek

Kings Canyon

THE RED CENTRE

Head of Kings Canyon

Road trains may be met on any outback road. These giant transports, consisting of a prime-mover linked to three trailers stretching for 50 metres (the cattle-trucks on more remote roads may have up to four trailers), are a dramatic sight — and a nightmare to pass on a narrow road. Fortunately the Stuart Highway is now a good wide road, but elsewhere there are many kilometres of narrow ribbons of bitumen that are too narrow to hold both a heavy transport and a car when passing. Either one or the other has to give way and move off the bitumen. The unwritten law is that at such times the transports have use of the whole bitumen, the lesser vehicle giving way and riding the road edges, however rough. This makes sense: nobody wants a speeding heavy transport to shower stones over their windscreen; and believe me, those monstrous vehicles can travel fast.

'Never argue with a road train,' a bloke in Alice Springs warned me, 'even if you think he's doing something that's beyond the limit of the law. And if you stop by the road, make sure you get well off it.' He went on to tell of the time when a motorist stopped to answer a call of nature, leaving his car on the side of the gravel road. Although he thought the car was parked safely enough, a road train didn't think so. When the man emerged from behind a tree, his car had gone. He later found it, now a mauled mass of iron, about a kilometre further along the road. So do take care.

George Gill Range at sunset

Hugh River

Devil's Marbles

Devil's Marbles at sunset

Wetlands, near Cooinda

TROPICAL OUTBACK

Many people believe that in no other part of Australia can the primeval quality of the land be felt so strongly as it is in the Northern Territory's tropical outback. You need spend only one night in the bush, and the distinctive atmosphere will pervade your senses. There is much beauty here, though visitors not familiar with the country often don't respond to it immediately — especially if they arrive travel-weary at their destination in the middle of the day, when the sun is high and hellishly hot. But spend only a few hours of the early morning or late afternoon around the rivers and lagoons, and the spirit of the place will touch you.

Like most travellers coming from the south via the Stuart Highway, I don't really feel I'm in the tropics until the Mataranka thermal pool is reached. Lying a comfortable day's drive from the Devil's Marbles, and just off the highway by the Mataranka Homestead resort, this beautiful pool, thickly fringed with lush tropical vegetation and fed by a natural spring, is a veritable oasis for tired tourists. The pool's water is 33°C, about the same as the day temperature. This may seem rather warm for swimming, but it is surprisingly refreshing. The water is also unusually clear, and every lichen-covered stone and twisted tree root, and every dancing watery rainbow cast by sunlight on the sandy bottom are all seen as if looking through spotlessly clean glass.

I best enjoy the pool in the stillness of dawn when few people are around; during the day it can get very crowded and noisy. However, on my last visit it seemed that everybody else from the nearby camping ground had the same idea, and at sunrise the pool hummed with swimmers. Memories flooded back of my first dawn swim, taken many years ago before the great tourist boom in the north. Nobody was around. It was an unusually chilly July morning, and the pool resembled a steaming cauldron, full of mood and mystery, as thick vaporous mists rose from the warm water and lazily drifted through the vegetation. Swimming in it was marvellous as it was like plunging into a huge hot bath; leaving the water was a different story: the air seemed more like 0°C than 10°C. Most winter mornings the pool is wreathed in some steam, but it takes exceptionally low atmospheric temperatures to produce the thick mist I saw that July dawn.

If the camping ground isn't too crowded, it is easy to stay an extra day or two at Mataranka. There is a pleasant walk along Waterhouse Creek to Steve's Pool, and tours run from the resort to the Roper River and its wetlands, and the surrounding district — now well-known through the book and film *We of the Never Never*. Mataranka is not far from a great attraction in the north: Katherine Gorge, in Nitmiluk National Park.

Lying near the town of Katherine, 312 kilometres south of Darwin, Katherine Gorge cuts through the southernmost reaches of the Arnhem Plateau in a series of thirteen gorges that imprison the Katherine River between high cliffs. Good walking trails run for many kilometres along the clifftops, but it is impossible to walk through the gorges because in many places the sheer walls plunge straight into the water.

Thermal pool, Mataranka

Katherine Gorge

TROPICAL OUTBACK

The best way to explore the gorges is by boat, and throughout the day a variety of two-hour trips go as far as the Grand Canyon at the end of the second gorge. The gorges are separated from each other by shallow rapids, but it is easy to walk around these to where a boat waits in the next gorge to take people on a further stage of the trip; not so easy is hauling a canoe over the rapids, but many people do it.

Over the years I have often taken the two-hour cruise, always preferring the first one for the day as the light is good for photography. However, the Johnstone's freshwater crocodiles are usually more plentiful in the afternoon, when the warm sun lures them to bask on rocks and branches of trees near the waterline. Often the boats can get quite close to them, though sometimes the smaller crocodiles are difficult to spot because of their excellent camouflage. These reptiles are harmless, and it is quite safe for swimmers to share the river with them.

My most memorable trip was the time I took the all-day safari. Although the boat carried us through five gorges, there was quite a lot of walking to do as we hiked over some large expanses of rocky rapids and through small patches of scrub. The July weather was ideal for walking, as a pleasant breeze kept the temperature down; the guide allowed plenty of time for swimming, a barbecue lunch and a walk to the beautiful lily pond lying off the third gorge. After the fifth gorge we scrambled up a cliff about sixty metres high and, after following a track along the top, cautiously peered over the precipitous side to view the equally grand sixth, seventh and eighth gorges. Far below lay the forlorn remains of a wrecked canoe, mute testimony to someone's unsuccessful attempt to negotiate the rapids.

In the Grand Canyon the boat went in very close to the splendid cliffs. Lush green ferns clung to the stark, rusty-red walls glowing with reflected light; some of the ferns protruded from the rocks like sprays of bright green feathers, while others spilled out of dim, moist grottoes. We also went in very close to some of the caves that overhung the water. As the boat approached, there was a flurry of wings and a cloud of fairy martins flew out from their bottle-shaped mud nests clustered on the cavern roof. Nearly every year they build there, only to have the results of their labours swept away by the river's raging floodwaters in the Wet.

Edith Falls, also part of Nitmiluk National Park, lie 20 kilometres off the Stuart Highway between Katherine and Pine Creek. Access is by a good bitumen road that leads to the camping ground set close to the spacious main pool that is fed by a small waterfall and backed by a craggy escarpment. Fortunately this inviting-looking pool is safe for swimming; above it there are more falls that cascade into a series of equally lovely rockholes.

On my first visit, I set off at sunrise to explore the other pools. Although it was the best time to be walking, the early morning light was not particularly good for photographing the falls and pools, so I returned later when the scenes were brilliantly lit by the afternoon sun. I had the place to myself (few people came here because the unsealed road was full of huge potholes and thick bulldust), and so I left the camera gear on a bank and climbed the rock face beside the waterfall, and swam up several pools linked by small rapids. One pool was bordered by a small sandy beach. It was heaven. Today I would not like to leave my camera equipment unattended as this has become a very popular place.

Edith Falls

Freshwater crocodile

Brolga

Umbrawarra Gorge is another small paradise, lying west of Pine Creek and only about 95 kilometres from Edith Falls. Access to this narrow but beautiful gorge is via an unsealed road that leads to a small camping area set near the creek that flows through the gorge. There is some delightful walking here, but progress is slow beyond the first gorge because time must be spent rock-hopping over the creek's tumbled rocks and boulders. I love the second gorge. Here, a long pool lies at the base of a high vertical wall that gives the place a special character of its own; at sunrise the wall flares a warm gold. Beyond the second gorge the rocks in the creek become huge chunky tors, and for further exploration, it is necessary to swim through some deep water.

It is easy to get a taste for exploring pools and waterfalls in the north. Once you get away from the good roads, the comfortable caravan parks and hotels, travelling by vehicle or on foot in hot weather through dusty and often rough scrub that offers little if any shade, can be hard. Weariness often kills the capacity to delight in the detail of land-scapes, and if you can find some water to splash away the heat, dust and fatigue, it will act as an exhilarating tonic for both mind and body, giving new energy to enjoy the remainder of the trip. However, the problem in northern Australia is to find a pool that is safe for swimming: many rivers, billabongs and lagoons are inhabited by saltwater crocodiles.

Popularly known as 'salties' and capable of growing over six metres in length, the saltwater or estuarine crocodile can be extremely dangerous both on land and in the water. Because of its highly attractive skin this reptile was threatened with extinction by hunters, but in 1971 it became fully protected. Since then, numbers have increased considerably. Attacks on people have increased, too — though it must be said that with nearly all the fatalities the victims invited trouble by doing something foolish.

Many popular tourist spots frequented by salties now have signs warning against swimming. If in doubt, always ask; and if there is nobody around to ask, play safe and cool yourself down with a bucket of water instead of a swim. Shallow rock pools, small running streams, and pools above waterfalls are always safe places. The closer you are to the coast, the more likely it is there will be crocodiles inhabiting the water. Although called a saltwater crocodile, the species can adapt to living in fresh water and has been known to move long distances inland. Fortunately there is now more public awareness of the dangers these awesome reptiles pose, and most people are generally very careful. I now shudder at some of the things I did years ago in crocodile country. On one occasion, before Kakadu was a national park, I waded across a section of Yellow Water Lagoon to get a better angle for a particularly promising photograph; today, boat tours take tourists out on that lagoon to see the salties! But then photographers are inclined to be rather daft.

Litchfield Park is one place in the Territory with some beautiful waterfall-fed pools that are safe for swimming: Wangi, Florence and Tolmer Falls are the most popular spots. Litchfield lies just west of the Stuart Highway, 110 kilometres from Darwin. Friends of mine in Darwin prefer Litchfield to Kakadu, but I have too many rich memories of Kakadu to make a comparison. I have only been to Litchfield once and liked it well enough, but it was hard to gain a favourable impression during a weekend when masses of people packed its pools.

Umbrawarra Gorge

Kakadu is one of Australia's major national parks, and has been accepted for inclusion on the prestigious World Heritage List. Covering a vast area, it lies about 250 kilometres east of Darwin at the edge of Arnhem Land. Access is via the bitumen Jabiru Highway from Darwin and the partly gravel road that runs from Pine Creek in the south. Kakadu is significant not only because it preserves a wealth of wildlife, scenic beauty and important natural features (almost the entire drainage basin of the great South Alligator River lies within the park), but also because of its rich heritage of Aboriginal culture.

Much of Kakadu's charm lies in its tropical wetlands, where a multitude of birds inhabit floodplains, rivers, lagoons, channels and billabongs that are fed by the heavy monsoonal rains between November and April. In striking contrast to the wetlands is the rugged Arnhem Land escarpment, a dominant feature in the east of the park. In many places deep, narrow gorges slice through the escarpment's old and worn sandstone cliffs; during the Wet, heavy rains cause thundering waterfalls to pour over their sheer walls, presenting fantastic spectacles when viewed from the air — the only way to see them then. At the edge of the escarpment lie many rocky outliers: some of the best-known are Nourlangie Rock, Ubirr, and Jabiru Dreaming. Many overhanging shelters of these outliers feature galleries of Aboriginal rock art, recognised as the finest of their type in the world. At Nourlangie Rock an excellent boardwalk has been built to enable visitors to view the art easily.

Brumbies

Florence Falls, Litchfield

I first visited Kakadu long before it was a national park in 1979, and since then I have witnessed a remarkable regeneration of the land — especially at Yellow Water Lagoon. Before 1979 the erosion caused by buffalo and wild pigs was frightful and many lagoons resembled bowls of thick brown soup where few waterlilies grew. A native of India, the buffalo was introduced from Timor during the early days of European settlement in northern Australia; when the first pioneering attempts failed, the beasts reverted to a wild state and rapidly multiplied in the swamplands east of Darwin, the area to which most of them were confined. Throughout the 1980s enormous herds were extensively culled — both in Kakadu and elsewhere — and today it is a rare sight to see one in the national park. Many people have mixed feelings about the extent of the culling, as the buffalo is a distinct symbol in the Territory, and despite its potential for being dangerous, is regarded with affection.

The feral pigs have been culled, too, though on my last visit I saw quite a few at Yellow Water. Few people mourn their dwindling numbers. The other feral animal motorists might see in the southern end of the park is the brumby (wild horse). They often run in mobs, and usually move off quickly at the sight of a car. On one occasion, I spotted some before they saw me, and I stopped the car and watched them frisking around the woodland. At first I thought they were fighting, but it was only a game, and as they cavorted through the trees with their shaggy manes flying and heads tossing, they seemed utterly carefree. These delightful animals are not popular with park rangers or station owners, because in large numbers they also damage the land. Descended from imported stock, many brumbies roaming the Australian bush are now inbred, and generally don't break in well for station work.

A highlight for visitors to Kakadu is Yellow Water Lagoon. Lying near Cooinda on the Pine Creek Road, this large lagoon and surrounding backwaters are fed by Jim Jim Creek. As the wetlands gradually shrink throughout the area during the dry season, Yellow Water resembles a giant outdoor aviary, full of many varieties of birds that come to feed in the permanent water. A long walkway stretches over a shallow backwater and provides excellent viewing over the lagoon; if you don't mind being eaten by mosquitoes, take a stroll along it at sunset, as the scenes can be breathtakingly beautiful. The best time of the day to be out on the lagoon in a boat is early morning or late afternoon — the latter is ideal to see the saltwater crocodiles. Boat tours run regularly throughout the day, and for wildlife enthusiasts and photographers, charter boats are available. Better still if you have your own boat.

On one visit, Lloyd and Audrey Cutler from Cooinda gave me a rare treat. When Lloyd wasn't skippering a commercial boat tour, he was out in his own boat with a camera. He not only knew all the species of birds at Yellow Water, but also knew what many of them were up to. 'There's a jacana that has some chicks,' he said to me one day. 'Would you like to come out with us and photograph them?' The jacana or lotus bird is an enchanting little creature renowned for walking on waterlily leaves. They also have an unusual habit of carrying their young under their wings, leaving the chicks' disproportionately long legs and toes dangling around the parent's body. I needed little persuading to see the jacana.

From Ubirr Lookout, Kakadu

Aboriginal rock art, Nourlangie Rock

TROPICAL OUTBACK

Yellow Water Lagoon

Sunset, Yellow Water Lagoon

Late that afternoon we went to an area well away from the route of the boat tours. Just before reaching a spot covered in waterlilies, Lloyd turned the boat's engines off and we drifted slowly in. Quietly he pointed out the jacana, a male, who was shepherding four fluffy plump chicks swimming in the water. As we drew closer, the bird quickly gathered them under his wings and continued to forage amongst the waterlilies. He was a co-operative little fellow and allowed us to get surprisingly close for photographs. Lloyd had his camera on a tripod balanced in the boat — he assured me the tripod was steady enough, providing we didn't wriggle. And that was not easy: every time I tried to rearrange my position for a better angle, the boat wobbled precariously. When that happened, Lloyd let out a growl that was directed not at the culprit but at Audrey, who sat like a statue for the entire photographic session. I thought it was rather noble of him to take another photographer.

The dry tropical woodlands are indeed a contrast to the magical, fecund wetlands. However, the seemingly monotonous woodlands do have their appeal early in the day, when the grasses release sweet pungent scents and the air is delectably cool. It doesn't take long for the land to loose its freshness once the sun climbs high in the sky. A diversion throughout the north's woodlands is the termite mounds. Rising from the ground like mud fortresses, the mounds vary from squat and knobbly creations to high, majestic towers. Their inhabitants make up the north's most powerful insect force and exert an enormous influence on the environment, devouring all types of vegetation; not even the trees escape. Termites eat out the trunks of many trees — much to the delight of the Aborigines, who turn some of these hollow trunks into the musical instruments known as didgeridoos.

During the dry season extensive areas of woodlands are often blackened by fire — a sight that disturbs many visitors. Although it is distressing to drive through recently scorched bush, the tough eucalypts, grasses and other plants of this region need the refining action of fire for their continuity — otherwise the prolific growth of vegetation would upset the present ecological balance. For centuries fire has controlled the far north's woodlands, most of the blazes being started by the Aborigines.

Nobody fights these fires, although in the national parks the burning is more controlled than elsewhere. The only extinguisher capable of putting them out properly is the first deluge of rain that falls towards the end of the Dry. As the vegetation dries out under the searingly hot sun, the fires increase in severity. Tourists making bush camps need to take care if the season is well advanced. Once, I was camping with friends and we had to break camp in a hurry because of fire. Everybody had been so engrossed in making camp that it was only when we sat down to enjoy a much-needed cold drink we became aware of an ominous crackling noise. To our horror we saw a fire leisurely approaching through the trees; there was no smell of smoke because the slight breeze was not blowing directly towards us. At other times I have watched lines of glowing flames that in the dark resemble an advancing army of beacon-carriers marching on the distant hills.

The top end of the Northern Territory has long been a favourite with visitors. However, with the phenomenal increase in 4WD vehicles and the inroads that tourism is making into remote areas, more people are exploring the region in far north-west Queensland lying south of the Gulf of Carpentaria, popularly known as the 'Gulf Country'.

Nourlangie Rock, from Sandy Billabong

Egret

Jacana carrying chicks

TROPICAL OUTBACK

The easiest but longer access to the Gulf Country from the Northern Territory is via the bitumen Barkly Highway, then travelling north from Camooweal or Cloncurry. A shorter route follows the Carpentaria Highway, starting from the Stuart Highway near Daly Waters, but a 4WD vehicle is recommended. After Borroloola, the bitumen road gives way to gravel, and once over the Queensland border it changes to a deeply rutted track pocked with alarming holes well-camouflaged by an ocean of bulldust that remains for most of the way to Burketown. Vehicles can bog in bulldust as well as mud, and when it happens to cattle-trucks it can be disastrous: unless the vehicles are extracted quickly, the stock will choke to death in the dust. When the trucks bog in mud, they may die of thirst.

The Burketown Shire Council has a dream that one day the road will be a proper highway linking the rest of Queensland with the Territory; but this is unlikely to happen as the Shire lacks money to upgrade it. 'No government is interested in us,' sighed one local. In the 1980s the Shire had an innovative idea: they approached the Defence Department and asked the army to upgrade the road in order to help the forces defend the north if ever it should be invaded. The Defence Department replied that it would be easier to check an advancing enemy if the road was left in its present condition.

My first trip across the Gulf Country was with a commercial safari, travelling in a vehicle that resembled a Unimog but had both sides open to the elements; every time another vehicle passed, billowing clouds of bulldust swept through our truck. Fortunately traffic was light, and when the dust had settled it was rather pleasant having natural air-conditioning blowing around us. With no windows, the vision was good and there was a heightened sense of being part of the scene.

We watched tropical woodland give way to broad open plains where seas of grass and vast claypans jostled for dominance. Small whirlwinds called willy-willies danced over the claypans in plumes of swirling dust, and brolgas roamed the grasslands, occasionally taking off in graceful flight. In places, clusters of termite mounds rose from the ground like a mass of graveyard headstones, their rich brown structures contrasting with the vivid yellow grass. Every afternoon the sky filled with masses of cottonwool clouds, giving an even deeper dimension to the scenes. In all directions there was a tremendous sense of distance: no wonder another name for this area is 'big sky country'.

Just west of Burketown lies Escott, a working cattle station that caters for fishermen and passing tourists. While we were there aerial flights were available, and so I took one. From the air the landscapes looked incredibly desolate, and I wondered how anybody could possibly exist in this country. Rough scrub gave way to endless areas of barren-looking plains and mudflats, many patterned with twisting rivers and their tributaries that nearer the coast displayed intriguing designs resembling trees and ferns. We flew over the mouth of the Nicholson River, its muddy waters disgorging into the Gulf. Our pilot was not keen to spend much time over the sea. 'We have only one engine,' he said, 'You would have little hope of surviving if the plane ditched in that drink — if the sharks didn't get you the crocs would. These waters are full of them.' I was glad I had taken the first flight for the day: the third one with the last of our group had barely taken off from Escott when the engine gave trouble, forcing them to return.

Burketown has a population of around 200. Situated on the Albert River not far from the coast, its residents like to think of Burketown as a port as there are only a few fishing boats here. However, only very small vessels can navigate the winding, mud-silted river.

Someone described Burketown as a town waiting for boom times — but it continues to wait in vain. We wandered around its scattered buildings, noting that the dominant architectural feature was galvanised-iron, and that the mongrel canine population seemed to outnumber the residents. At the river crossing just out of town a sign stated 'NO CAMPING' above a graphic drawing of a gaping croc's jaws. What a pity, we thought, it was hot and the water looked so inviting.

On our way to Lawn Hill Gorge, we stopped at the Gregory Downs Hotel — known as 'the Gregory Pub'. In what appeared to be the middle of nowhere, the pub rested at the junction of the Camooweal, Burketown, Lawn Hill and Julia Creek roads. Across an extraordinarily wide road from the pub stood a huge galvanised-iron edifice that was the local hall, used occasionally for dances and meetings. Apart from a couple of sheds and a few motel rooms resembling dog boxes near the hotel, that was the extent of the settlement; its population, we were told, was six people. The pub had been there since 1876.

Termite mound, tropical woodland

TROPICAL OUTBACK

Fire, tropical woodland

Aborigines making fire

We all trooped into the bar, which was also a store. While the others tucked into a surprising assortment of ice-creams and lollies, I looked hopefully for some fresh fruit. When I asked the barman if he had any bananas, he roared with laughter. 'Bananas!' He shouted. 'Lady, you're in the outback now. You can't expect things like that here!' I didn't think my request was unreasonable because bananas travel well; and the locals must eat some fresh produce. It was not as if I had asked for a peach!

While in the Gulf Country, most people go out of their way to visit Lawn Hill Gorge, lying 225 kilometres south-west of Burketown. The last 100 kilometres are rough, but suitable for 2WD vehicles. Five gorges confine Lawn Hill Creek, and all are lined with superb tropical vegetation; in the magnificent second gorge, colourful cliffs rise sheer from the water up to 60 metres. No motor boats are allowed in this national park, but canoes are available for hire. This place is a paradise for canoeists: between the second and third gorge an excellent canoe ramp enables them to take their craft easily over the rocks to the next gorge. From the camping ground at the second gorge, walking paths meander over the clifftops, giving many splendid views over the gorges and surrounding country.

Lying east of Burketown is Normanton, the largest town in the Gulf Country with a population of approximately 1100. A notice on the outskirts of town states 'Welcome to Normanton. Population — small. We love them all. Drive carefully.' It is easy enough to drive carefully down Normanton's very wide streets that are full of historic buildings — indeed, it is worth visiting this town just to see them. From Normanton a mostly bitumen road runs across the base of Cape York Peninsula to the east coast.

Escott Station, near Burketown

Aerial view of the Nicholson River, near Burketown

Lawn Hill Gorge

Cockburn Range and Pentecost River

THE NORTH-WEST

Some of the continent's most spectacular scenery lies in the State of Western Australia's north-west, yet it is only in comparatively recent times that the area has become accessible to the average tourist. Before the 1970s Australians knew very little about the remote Kimberley and Pilbara regions, but once mining roads pushed through and beef roads were upgraded, tourists soon followed. The roadwork continues.

Nearly twice the size of the State of Victoria, the Kimberley covers the vast north-west corner of Australia. Many people consider it to be the most exhilarating region in the country; indeed, I believe that few other areas in Australia can match its beauty and grandeur. One of the Earth's wildest places, the Kimberley is a world of rugged ranges, spectacular gorges, lush waterholes, broad plains, intriguing boab trees, and big rivers that flow only for a few months of the year.

Strictly speaking, the Kimberley is part of the tropical outback, as it has only two seasons, the Wet and the Dry. However, unlike the rest of tropical Australia, the temperatures are higher in summer and lower in winter — in July it is not uncommon for the nights to drop to 0°C. The best months for travelling are between May and September. Much potential enjoyment is lost if campers choose to be in the Kimberley's inland between the end of September and the start of the Wet in December, when temperatures can climb to over 40°C for days on end; these months are called the 'troppo' or 'suicide' season, because of the effects this humid heat has on people.

On my last trip to the Kimberley, in June, I decided to travel a popular route I call 'The Great Kimberley Loop': Kununurra to Derby via the gravel Gibb River Road, and return via the bitumen Great Northern Highway, a total of 1546 kilometres — not counting detours to gorges. At Kununurra I purchased enough supplies to last until Derby. Situated by Lake Kununurra on the Ord River and established in 1960 to serve the Ord River Irrigation Scheme, this pleasant town has the best shops and facilities in the far north-west; it is also the main town of the east Kimberley. Before taking the Gibb River Road turnoff lying between Kununurra and Wyndham, I detoured to Wyndham.

Set near the end of the Cambridge Gulf, the town is in two sections, Wyndham and Port Wyndham. Over the years some rather crude statements have been made about this place, as it has gained a reputation for being a bit of a dump; certainly in the 'troppo' season it is unbearably hot. But Wyndham has character. A little time is needed to discover it, but the more I visit the old Port area with its quaint historic buildings, the more I like it. The town nestles at the foot of a range called The Bastion, and from its summit the Five Rivers Lookout gives stunning views over the Cambridge Gulf and its surrounding mud and salt flats. I drove up to the lookout late afternoon, when the low sunlight softened the stark and forbidding landscapes, giving it a beauty not seen at other times of the day.

Along the Wyndham road stood some large and interesting boab trees that just begged to be photographed. They had lost their Wet season's covering of leaves, and revealed a collection of bare, untidy limbs that looked more like roots than branches.

I find boabs full of charm, and most entertaining. No two trees are the same: each has its own individual character. The young, slender ones are almost elegant, while the older trees, with their swollen and often split trunks, look distinctly arthritic and even grumpy; some are so grotesque they resemble warty old goblins. Confined to this corner of Australia, the boab is one of only two species, the other originating in Africa. Its more formal name on both continents is baobab, but Australians find this rather a mouthful and have shortened it.

Once the bitumen had been left behind for the stony Gibb River Road, I travelled more slowly — not just for the vehicle's sake, but it was easier to drink in the beauty of the countryside. Although a 4WD vehicle is recommended, once the grader has been over the road at the start of the dry season it is suitable for 2WDs — but only just, as there are some very rough sections. In the past I have taken a Hiace campervan through without any trouble, but access to some of the many gorges was limited.

Someone once likened the Kimberley's gorges to visiting cathedrals in Europe: there are so many of them that you get scenic indigestion. I disagree, because each gorge here is so different from every other — and the last one visited is always the best. The first gorge I called to see was Chamberlain Gorge, on El Questro Station. The young English owner was preparing for a big cattle muster, but despite all the activity, he assured me that visitors are always welcome. He directed me to some of the most shady and idyllic camp sites I have seen in the Kimberley; they lay along the creek near the very impressive gorge, and I found it a hard place to leave.

A prominent feature along the Gibb River Road's eastern end is the Cockburn Range, a huge plateau-topped massif wearing fantastic collars of pinky-brown rock. The road runs beside it for many kilometres, leaving it at a particularly scenic area at the Pentecost River crossing. I knew crocodiles inhabited the Pentecost, so I didn't want to linger. However, photographing it took longer than planned because a stubborn cloud stayed over the late afternoon sun for nearly an hour. I didn't feel very comfortable waiting for that length of time by my camera set on the tripod at the water's edge. Eventually it did come out, and the brooding Cockburn Range, now swathed in shades of pink and red, provided a marvellous backdrop for the river. Later, Ian Sinnamon at Home Valley Station advised me not to hang around the water's edge again for any lengthy periods. 'There are some very big and aggressive crocs in that river,' he said.

Home Valley Station lies on the western side of the Pentecost River. They also welcome visitors, and offer some good tours. I stayed a night at the station's lodge, and enjoyed one of their delightful baronial-style dinners by candlelight; this made a pleasant change from opening a can of something and sleeping in the camper. The station also has a lodge and camping ground at Jack's Waterhole, a large permanent pool on the Durack River about an hour's drive further on.

The rather uninteresting 200 kilometres between Jack's Waterhole and Mount Barnett Station were as bone-jarring as ever, however some patches of new road relieved the rough driving. It was on this bad section of road, back in 1980, that I met a group of young men from Britain and France who had run out of petrol; it also appeared they had little water and food in their battered-looking Holden station-wagon. They had not re-fuelled at Kununurra — or checked the location of the next petrol station. In those days there was little traffic on the road, and fuel was only available at Mount Barnett Station, 403 kilometres from Kununurra. As I had plenty of extra fuel I gave them some. Today, petrol is available at Jack's Waterhole and Mount Barnett, and there is a lot of traffic on the road — but there are plenty of other outback roads that could claim lives if motorists are not properly prepared.

Lake Argyle at the Ord Dam

THE NORTH-WEST

Boab tree, near Wyndham

From the Five Rivers Lookout, Wyndham

Some gorges lie near Mount Barnett Station: Barnett, Manning, Adcock and Galvans Gorges. Access from carparks is by foot; and they all have rockpools that are suitable for swimming, providing much-needed refreshment in the heat. After briefly calling into these gorges I pressed on towards a gorge I had wanted to see for years: Bell Gorge. Now that I had a 4WD vehicle I could do so.

Before 1986 few people had heard of this gorge. It lies on Silent Grove Station, and it is only in recent years the station has permitted people to visit it. Everyone I met who had been there raved about the place; indeed, one guide book declared that if you visit only one gorge in the Kimberley, make it Bell Gorge. It took me two hours to negotiate the 29 extremely rough kilometres from the Silent Grove turnoff to the end of the track at the top of a hill; turning the vehicle wasn't easy on the narrow track as huge rocks studded the ground. On the way in I had passed fourteen vehicles; what a relief to find only one parked at the track's end! From there it was a twenty minute walk to the gorge.

A large bell carved in the trunk of a slender boab marked the start of the track that went down the hill; and once at the creek, little piles of stones guided the way to the top of the falls and its pool. Never having seen a photograph of this place I didn't know what to expect. It was larger than I had imagined, and only when I scrambled up its rocky slopes near the top of the waterfall and walked around the top could the full extent of its grandeur be appreciated. Well before sunset I had to gallop up the hill to the vehicle to get more film.

Soon after leaving Silent Grove, the Gibb River Road winds through the wildly beautiful King Leopold Range. I gave Lennard Gorge a miss because a few years earlier I had got halfway in with my Hiace, and discovered the rest of the track was so bad it was barely fit for a 4WD vehicle. I had heard that this dramatic gorge was unusually rugged, and if you did manage to get to it either by vehicle or on foot you would need to be a mountain goat to climb down into it.

The next gorge I visited was one of my favourites: Windjana Gorge. A national park lying in the Napier Range 25 kilometres off the Gibb River Road and only 150 kilometres from Derby, Windjana is one of the most impressive of the well-known gorges in the Kimberley. There is a sense of space here, which in no way lessens the splendour of the orange-splashed grey walls that rise like a mighty fortress to 90 metres above the plain.

I walked through the gorge early in the morning. It was too early to see the freshwater crocodiles that lived in the pool by the large white rock, about a kilometre from the entrance. However, there were plenty of birds around: flocks of white corellas and galahs wheeled in the air, their shrill cries echoing loudly around the range. Between their screeching, I picked up the sound of a great bower-bird in a nearby tree. Sure enough, there was a bower of sticks on the ground, and I waited quietly in some nearby bushes for the male to come down to it. It wasn't long before he appeared. After inspecting the collection of stones, shells and berries that formed a mat at the entrance to the bower's avenue, he selected a choice twig and carefully placed it in the wall. For about an hour I watched him make more improvements to the bower.

Windjana Gorge is a good place to see some Wandjina rock art. Considerable mystery surrounds the Wandjina paintings that are found throughout the Kimberley. Although for generations the Aborigines have ritually touched up these strange mouthless figures wearing haloes, they were not the original artists. Local legends say the Wandjinas were Dreamtime supermen who came from the north-west, and on their death they assumed the form of rock paintings. It is a four-hour walk to the ones in Windjana Gorge; the finest ones I have seen in the Kimberley were on the north-west coast.

Bell Gorge Falls

THE NORTH-WEST

Windjana Gorge

On this visit I did not go on to Tunnel Creek, an hour's drive from Windjana. It is the sort of place you need to explore with other people, as it is very spooky walking through the 750-metre-long cave that pierces the range. Good torches are necessary, and be prepared to meet the odd python and possibly to wade through chest-high, icy-cold water. Some years ago I walked through with friends, but as it was late in the dry season, we only got our ankles wet. The best part was seeing the collapse in the cave, lying half-way through; it also gave a respite from the inky blackness that seemed to reduce our strong Big Jim torches to the effectiveness of a few pathetic candles.

After refuelling at Derby, I picked up the Great Northern Highway to head back east. At Fitzroy Crossing, a highway settlement 260 kilometres from Derby, I drove out to nearby Geikie Gorge. Probably the best-known gorge in the region, Geikie borders the Fitzroy River for eight kilometres and is the major feature in a small national park. Like Windjana Gorge and Tunnel Creek, it lies in the limestone ranges that were part of the ancient Devonian 'Great Barrier Reef', formed in a past era when part of the Kimberley was covered by tropical seas. In the walls of these imposing narrow ranges that wind over the country for 300 kilometres are many well-preserved fossils that show the animals and plants of the prehistoric sea.

The cave-in, Tunnel Creek

As access to Geikie is very easy, most coaches touring the Kimberley bring their passengers here for a boat tour. I joined the afternoon tour. Running only in the dry season, these tours are made aboard a series of flat-bottomed boats strung together, and the ranger skilfully guides this unusual craft close to the walls of the gorge, enabling you to appreciate fully the detail of the incredible markings, indentations and holes that riddle sections of the cliffs. The walls' other outstanding feature is their brilliant colouring: in many places a multitude of warm shades seems to have been splashed on with a paintbrush. I prefer the afternoon tour because then these colours are at their most vibrant.

The next afternoon I decided to take the walk along the western bank and see Geikie's colourful walls at sunset reflecting in the Fitzroy River. Laden with camera gear, the half-hour walk to the best section of cliffs nearly killed me on that hot afternoon, as it was a hard plod over the wide expanse of very loose sand lying between the cliffs and the river's edge. Every time I do this walk I vow never to do it again — but I always come back. By the time I had caught my breath under a shady tree by the river, the breezes dropped and I joyously photographed the wonderful scene. Camping is no longer permitted in this national park, but there are camping grounds and a motel at Fitzroy Crossing.

Before returning to Kununurra, there was one important national park to visit: the Bungle Bungle Range. Few places have stirred such interest in recent times as its 'discovery' by an aerial film crew in 1983; until then, only the Aborigines and some pastoralists knew it existed. So little was known about it that when the range was first publicised, one government official in Canberra faxed a colleague to ask if he had heard of Bungle Bungle. The return fax read: 'No. Sounds like the name of a government department.' It is astonishing that such a geological masterpiece — and one of Australia's most extraordinary landscapes — could remain virtually unknown for so long, but the wild Kimberley region is ideal for keeping secrets.

Declared a national park in 1987, the Aborigines know it as Pernululu, while many Europeans prefer to call it 'the Bungles'. Rising from the plains as a great triangular massif, the range is cut by ravines and edged by high cliffs that in places reach 400 metres and give way to masses of weathered-orange and black-banded domes said to be the most dramatic examples of their type on Earth. It is these beehive-like formations that visitors come to see.

The range lies 55 kilometres off the highway. Although the track to the park has been upgraded in recent years, it is still very rough and remains strictly for 4WD vehicles. On previous visits I had to rely on commercial tours to show me the place; with my own 4WD, I could spend as much time as I liked taking photographs without driving other people nuts. So with considerable anticipation I left the highway 100 kilometres north of Halls Creek for the Bungles. My joy was short-lived: the vehicle had travelled only a few kilometres on the rough track when to my horror I saw the front bullbars lurch then drop off the vehicle. What to do? Nobody was around. I had no choice but to heave them into the camper section of the vehicle and continue my journey. I didn't want to return to Halls Creek, so for the next few days, every time I wanted a meal or a cuppa I had to pull the large bullbars out of my living quarters. It was not the rough roads that had caused them to fall off: the wrong bolts had been used in the installation.

Wandjina rock painting

Great bower-bird and bower

Willy-willy (whirlwind)

Geikie Gorge

Echidna Chasm

Like most people, I chose to camp at the picturesque Kurrajong camp on the north-west side of the range. The lack of domes in this part of the park comes as a surprise to some people, who expect to see nothing but domes everywhere. The range becomes more 'Bungleoid' in appearance further south — but it offers more to see than just beehive-like domes. Echidna Chasm lies just north of Kurrajong. I waited till midday to explore this incredibly narrow and deep ravine that sees little sun. At that hour the partially lit, red-brown walls provided a perfect backdrop for the dark shapes of the many ancient *Livistona* palms growing there. Dead fronds crackled loudly underfoot as I made my way through the chasm which narrowed to a metre near its end. Not counting photo stops, the walk took about thirty minutes.

There were more palms in Frog Hole, another gorge lying near Echidna Chasm. Frog Hole is more open than Echidna Chasm, and with its towering walls and huge chunky boulders it is easy to see the immensity of the Bungles' massif. After exploring Frog Hole I drove to Piccaninny Creek at the southern end of the park to see the domes.

Outcrop of domes, Bungle Bungle Range

THE NORTH-WEST

It took about an hour from Kurrajong to reach the first outcrops of domes. I had been warned that the sand was very loose and deep along the sloping stretch by the outcrop known as the 'Bull Elephant', and that the track was riddled with speed traps but actually were water spreads to stop water erosion during the Wet. As I wanted to photograph this fascinating outcrop, I chose my parking spot with care. From here, it took a long time to reach the Piccaninny Creek carpark; it wasn't so much the rough track that slowed me down as the scenery: domed formations were everywhere, standing in sausage-like clumps or appearing as part of the range — which in places displayed a million little hills piled high upon each other. After leaving the vehicle at the carpark I walked into Piccaninny Creek and was surrounded by more domes.

The ultimate experience in the Bungles is a helicopter flight. In the past I had taken various fixed wing flights from Kununurra and Halls Creek that were excellent — but they cannot be compared with one in a chopper. These flights are now so popular that Slingsby Helicopters keeps a pilot and a machine stationed at the Kurrajong camp throughout the tourist season. As I have learnt from experience that tourists and photographers don't mix well on a flight if the doors are off the machine, I went alone, at sunrise.

Aerial view of domes, Bungle Bungle Range

Bungle Bungle massif, Horseshoe Valley

In Piccaninny Creek

THE NORTH-WEST

It is not until you see this place from a close-range aerial perspective that the full extent of the Bungles' wild and rugged terrain can be appreciated. As we flew over the massif's plateau, eroded bluffs rolled on and on, giving way to steep gullies and sheer ravines where palms and other vegetation appeared to be rooted in impossibly rough ground. Once out in the spacious Horseshoe Valley area on the eastern side, I looked with awe at the great walls, now flaring gold in the first light of the sun as it rose above the sparsely tree-studded plain. Then we flew over the southern end, where the masses of domes looked like a vast array of conical pots spread over the plain. It was breathtaking.

Both doors were off the chopper; this may have been perfect for taking photographs, but with a stiff wind blowing through the machine it was a nightmare changing films. For most of the flight I had the distinct feeling I could be blown out at any moment; at one point I nearly lost the camera bag but managed to catch it in time. The next morning I took another flight and requested that one door be left on — and that proved to be ideal.

I left the Bungles and rejoined the highway, content that at long last I had been able to see the place under my own steam. However, when the most appalling noise of metal striking bitumen suddenly erupted from the back of my one-year-old 4WD, I began to think there might be a few advantages after all in travelling with commercial tours. With a sinking heart I stopped the vehicle and discovered that the camper's water-tank had broken loose. Dribbling out water, it was still attached to the vehicle by a longish plastic pipe that resembled an umbilical cord belonging to some strange metal foetus. After cutting the pipe I saved some of the water in a spare jerry can, then heaved the empty tank into the camper and lived with it for the next fortnight until repairs under warranty could be done in Melbourne. The rough roads had been too much for the brackets supporting the tank.

Western Australia's other outback area of great scenic significance is the Pilbara. Photographically, I believe it to be the most colourful in Australia. However, despite its dramatic scenery, somehow I find it lacks the appealing atmosphere found in the Kimberley. It may be the Pilbara's harsh conditions, though at times in the Kimberley I have photographed under much more difficult circumstances.

Lying south-west of the Kimberley and separated by the Great Sandy Desert, the Pilbara spreads inland from the coast between Roebourne and Port Hedland to the eastern edge of the desert. Little rain falls here, and in summer the temperatures soar to around 49°C. The town of Marble Bar has some of the highest recorded temperatures in the country, and just the thought of their longest heatwave is enough to make any southerner melt: for 160 days in 1923–24 the temperature did not drop below 37°C. 'The summers are hell,' one woman told me in Wittenoom. 'At times the heat is almost unbearable, and when the dust storms hit the town, the airconditioning usually breaks down. We get a lot of dry electrical storms, too. They are scary as you keep hearing loud bangs as the lightning strikes things, and it seems to dance along the ironstone range.'

In winter the climate is bearable, and that is the time to visit. Like most who live in south-eastern Australia, I find the Pilbara one of the hardest regions to reach, because of the distance involved and the travelling time required. From my home in Victoria to the Hamersley Range it is some 4540 kilometres. Because it is ironstone country, the unsealed roads are among the stoniest in Australia, and I have learnt from hard experience to drive slowly here to minimise the risk of getting punctures. On one visit, I was told that the road running from the mining town of Tom Price to the coast was known as 'The Six Weeks Grade': it was so bad that it required grading every six weeks, and even that, according to the locals, wasn't often enough. My informant reckoned that the grader went over it most of the time with the blade up. The Pilbara is also an awful place for dust, especially for campers: brightly rust-coloured, it gets into everything and leaves you feeling permanently grubby — even after washing. Everything you touch seems to be covered with it.

Hamersley Range, near Wittenoom

THE NORTH-WEST

I usually come to the Pilbara from the Kimberley, and from Port Hedland take the bitumen road to Wittenoom, at the foot of the Hamersley Range. Once I took the unsealed road through Marble Bar, and cut across some very interesting country to pick up the Port Hedland road. But the signposting was poor, and my maps gave me no help, and if it hadn't been for a grader driver I met, I would have wasted a lot of petrol wandering around the bush.

The iron ore-rich Hamersley Range stretches for nearly 400 kilometres across the Pilbara. Part of the range is a national park that protects a series of deep and richly coloured gorges fissuring the plateau that tops it. Unsealed roads lead up to the plateau, the camping grounds and the gorges with their terraced walls of chocolate, red and rust that are accentuated by the pristine white trunks of gums, and the lush vegetation beside the pools of water lying far below. Although there is access into some of the gorges, most visitors view them from above. There are no guard-rails, and this can be a terrifying experience for people who don't like heights, for in some places the sheer walls plummet 150 metres. Kinder to the senses are the landscapes around Wittenoom. If the seasonal rains have been good, the wildflowers splash even more colour around, and sometimes great candelabras of mulla mullas carpet the plains right up to the folds of the range.

The Hamersley Range may be the main draw-card for visitors to the Pilbara, but to the north lies another notable place: the Chichester Range, 180 kilometres from Wittenoom. I call this 'painted desert' country: rust, pink, and chocolate-hued rocks dominate the landscape, and the ridgetops are so littered with them that it seems as if a giant tiptruck has been at work among the golden domes of spinifex. The Roebourne Road runs over the range; below, there is access to Python Pool and a camping ground. I always like to spend a night here because at sunrise the high rocky walls around the pool blaze briefly as if on fire, spilling red and then orange colours over the water.

The Chichester Range is part of the Millstream-Chichester National Park. At Millstream a long lily-covered pool, flanked by paperbarks and a unique species of *Livistona* palm, wells from a natural spring and flows into the Fortescue River. The river's permanent pools are also lined with lush vegetation, and along its banks there are some wonderful spots for camping. Shade and water are rare commodities in the Pilbara, and both Millstream and the Fortescue River provide a refreshing antidote for the heat and dust. I always spend more days here than planned, and then find it very hard to break camp.

It was in the Pilbara that I once saw a rare phenomenon: for want of a better name, I called it a moonbow. An unseasonal shower had just passed, and a full moon hung above the eastern horizon. In the west, where a heavy bank of rain clouds lay, appeared a great white bow with both ends touching the plains. Except for its colour, it looked like a rainbow. Against the dark clouds it was an amazing sight; but it stayed only briefly before it gradually faded into the night. Later, I learnt that nocturnal rainbows contain the same colours as daytime ones, but the eye doesn't detect them at such a low light intensity.

Fortescue River, near Millstream

Python Pool, Chichester Range

Kalamina Gorge, Hamersley Range

Snappy gum, Yampire Gorge, Hamersley Range

THE NORTH-WEST

From Mount Romilly, Great Sandy Desert

THE DESERTS

THE DESERTS

There are six major deserts in outback Australia: the Simpson, Sturt, Tanami, Great Victoria, Gibson and Great Sandy deserts. The last three join to form by far the greatest expanse of arid land, covering a large portion of Western Australia and running into South Australia.

These deserts have become a challenge for a growing number of 4WD enthusiasts, who will cheerfully spend months planning a journey across vast seas of dunes, empty gibber wastes and arid lands studded with clay and salt pans that can be treacherous after rain. Such journeys must be well prepared because these forbidding regions have claimed many lives over the years. It is essential to carry a good radio transmitter and, for most deserts, enough provisions, water and fuel for the entire journey. Except in the Tanami and Gibson, there are no settlements or proper roads.

The Simpson Desert spreads into parts of South Australia, the Northern Territory and Queensland. Its dominant feature is lines of unbroken dunes lying like great ribs across the dry plain; unlike the Sahara Desert, these dunes are not of the constantly shifting type, but are fixed longitudinal ridges that rise to heights of up to 45 metres. Because the western aspect of each dune slopes gently to the crest before dropping steeply on the other side, vehicular crossings are usually made from west to east.

Of all the deserts, the Simpson is my favourite. My first experience of it was on a day excursion out from Alice Springs to a great sight of the outback: Chambers Pillar, lying at the desert's edge, 125 kilometres south-east of Alice Springs. From this solitary monolith's massive stony pedestal, a fluted column of sandstone rears 30 metres above the red sandy plains, dwarfing everything in its proximity. Since its discovery in 1860, it has been a landmark for explorers and surveyors. The explorer Ernest Giles poetically described it as 'a vast monument in its loneliness and grandeur, mystic and wonderful'. To be less romantic, any modern-day visitor who has had an association with the navy, will declare that it bears a striking resemblance to the conning tower of a submarine.

My first trip to the Pillar in 1975 was a memorable one. A car dealer in Alice Springs had been keen to see how the newly released 4WD Subaru performed in rough terrain, and I was invited to join the group. With some misgivings I piled into the Subaru that looked more suitable for city suburbs than the desert; our escort vehicle looked even less robust: a peculiar looking contraption that bore some resemblance to a Volkswagen Beetle but was called a beach buggy. Four hours later we arrived safely; the Subaru had handled the dunes superbly, but couldn't carry its heavy load of five adults over the high and very steep rocky range lying just before the start of the dunes. When four of us got out and walked up, the vehicle breezed over it.

One look at the Pillar and I knew that it had to be photographed at sunrise or sunset. It was most frustrating not being able to spend a night there. My second trip was the same: again I spent only a few hours there at midday, as I was on a commercial tour on the way back from an aborted crossing of the desert because of rain. I had to wait many years to see it at sunset, and when I eventually got my own 4WD vehicle, the first place I headed for was Chambers Pillar. For three mornings and nights I photographed it when the sun stood poised on the horizon, its low light causing the Pillar to appear like a flaming beacon; it was just as thrilling seeing it silhouetted against the evening sky, after sunset.

I first crossed the Simpson with Desert-Trek Australia. The tour left from Adelaide, where we boarded a Toyota Landcruiser fitted with radial sand tyres, extra petrol tanks and a sophisticated radio transmitter, and entered the desert via Oodnadatta and Dalhousie. The route was little more than a set of wheel tracks.

About 30 kilometres after driving over the first dune, we stopped at Purni Bore. Water filled several pools, but it was the area around the borehead that held our attention. Purni's water is so laden with minerals that in and around the pools colourful deposits had hardened into ridges, shelves, and fantastic formations, including a metre-high weird

Chambers Pillar at sunset

hood around the borehead that noisily spouted steaming water. With extreme care we walked to the borehead, trying to avoid the treacherously slippery spots — a fall into a hot pool didn't bear thinking about. Later I learnt that we had been fortunate: on another tour, the ground near the borehead crumbled beneath the weight of one man and he fell in. His burns were so severe that he had to be taken out by the Flying Doctor.

We spent four nights in the desert. Strangely enough we never tired of the dunes: always there was the anticipation of what lay in the next valley. From the top of the higher dunes, a sea of sand-hills undulated towards the horizon like ocean waves, their crests splashed with bare patches of red; at sunset they turned the colour of blood. The distance between dunes was anything up to a kilometre.

As there had been several years of good rains, many plants were well established. Gradually the vegetation changed: forests of acacias gave way to grevilleas, cassias, a host of smaller plants — and the eternal spinifex. Many plants were in flower, giving the effect of a wild garden. Above all, there was the impact of colour. Set against a cloudless blue sky, the vivid red sand seemed like an artist's palette splashed with all the different greens of the foliage and the colours of the flowers, especially the golden clouds of acacia blooms.

Chambers Pillar after sunset

THE DESERTS

We travelled slowly, and so it was easy to absorb the desert's beauty. Within all the untrammelled growth of this wilderness, we delighted in absorbing the infinite variety of details and letting our eyes linger over a lovely flowering plant, the windblown ripple patterns in a bare stretch of sand, or the intricate designs of animal tracks. The desert appeared to support plenty of living creatures. Dingoes were openly curious. I had heard some strange stories about them in the Simpson: the one I liked least was about the man who woke to find one sniffing his face. The dingo may have showed no fear, but the man was terrified. We encountered quite a variety of wildlife: there were many birds, including emus, bustards (wild turkeys), and wedge-tailed eagles. Of the reptiles, we sighted a perentie, and many bearded dragons. Once a large mob of brumbies galloped across our track; but we saw no camels, which was unusual.

For the entire crossing the August days were fine and mild, but the nights under star-studded heavens were cold, mostly around or below freezing. I had been warned they could be exceptionally cold, with temperatures tumbling to as low as −12°C. At night the awesome silence was occasionally briefly broken by the twittering of a night bird or the howl of a dingo, the sounds coming through with astounding clarity. Noises around our campsite were magnified too, and I felt compelled not to make too much clatter — almost as if I were in a cathedral. One night we were startled by what sounded like an oncoming truck just beyond the next dune, but it was only a passing jet, high in the sky.

As we drew closer to the borders of the three States, we came to the first of many salt lakes that lie between the red dunes like white dishes, smooth and inviting for drivers. After rain the hard crust gives way to water, which may lie for months under a newly formed crust — and this can be a real problem for motorists. We had no trouble driving over the first salt lake, but it was a different story with the large one lying beside some rocky hills with the impossible name of Approdinna Attora Knolls which our driver wanted to show us.

We never reached the Knolls. Quite suddenly the wheels of our vehicle started to sink through the white salty crust which up till then had been providing a very hard road. After surveying our hopelessly bogged vehicle, we walked to the edge of the lake to collect piles of dead bushes that smelt unpleasantly of stale salt. These were packed into the deep wheel ruts to give traction to the wheels, but when attempting to drive out, the vehicle just sank deeper. To our horror, we watched it settle into liquid that looked very much as if it belonged to the water-table lying underneath the surface. After taking everything out of the vehicle we somehow managed to shove underneath it a stack of old gidgee branches, and then drive out. While we worked the wind freshened and whipped up whirl-winds of salt; apprehensively we watched the tall white columns dancing over the lake, but they stayed away from us.

Probably the best known spot is Poeppel's Corner, where the three State borders meet. The point is marked by a large concrete peg, surrounded by an extraordinary array of plaques erected mostly by members of 4WD clubs. To our astonishment there was even a visitors' book, kept in a neat steel container. At the beginning of the book there was an interesting historical account of the desert, and we reflected on the stalwart men who had blazed trails over the Simpson: Colson's first crossing of the desert's southern portion by camel in 1936, followed by Madigan's official one in 1939 (also by camel). Madigan had commented 'This is one place where the motor vehicle will never penetrate.' The first vehicular crossing was made by Reg Sprigg in 1962. Today, if you drive through it during a winter school holiday period, the now well-worn track may resemble a busy city road.

Purni Bore, Simpson Desert

Dingo

Young wedge-tailed eagle

Dune, Simpson Desert

THE DESERTS

<hr />

Shortly after Eyre Creek, we crossed the highest dunes of the trip. The highest, known as 'Big Red' and presenting a big test for drivers, was topped with a massive crest of bare, drifting sand. Without too much drama, and using every rev the vehicle could muster, we roared over it and, after crossing the Diamantina River's wide and utterly featureless floodplain, headed for a famous watering hole, the Birdsville pub.

The Simpson Desert gives way to Sturt's Stony Desert, which lies chiefly between the Diamantina River and Cooper Creek in north-eastern South Australia. It is probably the grimmest of the continent's deserts, and one is not surprised to hear that when the explorer Charles Sturt made the first crossing of this inhospitable area in 1845 he commented that it was 'A country such as I firmly believe has no parallel on the Earth's surface.' Vast seas of gibbers, varying in size from tiny pebbles to large stones, give way in a few places to areas of spinifex and sand-dunes. The Birdsville Track runs through its western edge, linking the settlements of Marree and Birdsville; and on its eastern edge a minor track runs through Cordillo Downs to Innamincka.

Moonrise, Simpson Desert

Crossing the heart of Sturt's Stony Desert must be made with the aid of a compass — and even then navigation can be difficult because of the nature of the terrain. I crossed this desert after completing another trip through the Simpson with Desert-Trek; instead of returning home via the Birdsville Track, we headed south-east through the Sturt shortly after leaving Birdsville. In some places wheelmarks ran in all directions, and we were grateful for the compass, especially when picking up grid-like seismic tracks. Surprisingly, there was a fascinating beauty in this desert's desolation: the play of light on the harsh gibbers stretching to the far horizon changed them from hard steel greys to deep warm reds, creating unusual scenes. It was an uneventful crossing, and we were all sorry to arrive at Innamincka. The desert had been so peaceful.

The next major desert expedition I made was through Western Australia's three deserts: the Great Victoria, the Gibson, and the Great Sandy deserts. We only touched the northern end of the Great Victoria near the Giles weather station, as most of the time was spent in the other two while travelling the historic Canning Stock Route. I joined one of Russell Guest's 4WD Safaris that escorted people in their own vehicles across remote areas of the outback. By now I had my own 4WD, but after hearing how difficult some of the driving could be in the Great Sandy Desert, I opted to ride in one of their escort vehicles. Even as a passenger, I learnt more about 4WD vehicles during this three-week trip than I had in the past year, as Russell and his co-drivers shared their desert-driving skills and mechanical knowledge with all the participants.

Our party of eleven vehicles headed west from Ayers Rock, and travelled a formed dirt road through the Gibson Desert to Carnegie Station, lying at the end of the Gunbarrel Highway, over 1100 kilometres from the Rock. The Gunbarrel was pushed through in 1963 — before that no road linked central Australia to the West. It may be called a highway, but it is just a very rough outback road; but then anyone travelling Australia will soon discover that if a route is labelled a highway, that doesn't necessarily mean it is a good road! I was surprised to see service stations at Giles and Warburton; the latter had a store that even sold fresh fruit. More people are now coming this way. However, permits are required by the Aboriginal Land Council to travel part of it — without them, you risk heavy fines.

Before reaching the end of the Gunbarrel Highway at Carnegie, the Gibson Desert featured rough scrub that gave way to the odd rocky hill and plains carpeted with wildflowers, watered by the best rains that had fallen for twelve years. I soon discovered that every time I requested a photo stop, the entire convoy came to a halt — as it did when anyone had a flat tyre or other troubles. Fortunately there was usually plenty of time to explore the desert around the camp late afternoon or early morning. All the vehicles were linked by CB radio, and Russell maintained some strict safety rules. One of them was that we had to be very careful not to wander alone too far from the camp or the track, because in the desert, where scrub and dunes can have a sameness for many square kilometres, it is very easy to get disoriented and loose your sense of direction. One person learnt this the hard way.

It happened early in the trip. I woke at first light to hear the sound of a man's voice ringing through the scrub. Every few minutes the call came from a direction where nobody was camped, and like everyone else, I thought it was someone fooling around. However, once Russell surfaced from his swag, he knew that someone was in trouble, and went after him. It turned out that a bloke had left his tent for a call of nature, and in the dark walked too far into the scrub, then couldn't find his way back to the tent. We were appalled to learn that the poor fellow had been roaming around totally disorientated for nearly an hour before he was brought back to camp.

Sturt's Stony Desert

Sturt's Stony Desert

Convoy, Gibson Desert

One of the Gravity Lakes, Great Sandy Desert

We joined the Canning Stock Route at Well 9, and headed north, leaving civilisation far behind. For over 1500 kilometres, and taking thirteen days, we journeyed through sand and spinifex that gave way at times to stony areas and the odd rocky hill and range. Russell pointed out that the Canning is the world's longest and loneliest drive through one country, not counting Siberia. It passes through no settlements, there are no petrol stations (travellers must arrange drums of petrol to be dropped at Well 23 from Newman, about 400 kilometres away). There isn't even much visible wildlife. Only a few of the 51 wells along the route have good water.

The longest stock route in Australia, the Canning runs for more than 1700 kilometres through the Gibson and Great Sandy Deserts to the Tanami Desert in the north. It was established by the surveyor Alfred Canning who, between 1907 and 1910 sank 52 wells at about 30 kilometres apart (a day's travel for cattle) between Wiluna in the south and Halls Creek in the Kimberley.

Well 10, Canning Stock Route

Canning Stock Route

Camel bones, Well 42

THE DESERTS

Durba Hills, Canning Stock Route

Lake Disappointment, Canning Stock Route

The purpose of the Canning Stock Route was to bring cattle from the east Kimberley to the railhead at Wiluna and thence to markets in Perth. At that time, a plague of cattle-ticks had infected stock throughout the east Kimberley to such a degree that the WA government restricted the movement of tick-infected cattle to other areas of the State. Kimberley cattlemen, now desperate for access to southern markets, asked the government to find an overland route through the arid inland, because as the tick only thrived in humid conditions, it would die while the cattle walked through the dry country of the proposed stock route.

The last cattle drive was in 1958. Ravaged by the elements, the route virtually disappeared over the years and a compass was an essential requirement for the few people who travelled it. The first vehicular crossing of the entire stock route was made in 1968 by two surveyors from Canberra. In 1976 about five vehicles travelled it; by the late 1980s it had become one of the last great challenges for 4WD adventurers, with over 500 vehicles going up or down it. That number increases each year. Today, it is a sign-posted, well-defined track, but only people who are extremely well-prepared and have suitable 4WDs should undertake the journey during the cooler months of the year. It is no place to be in at the height of the summer.

Most days we covered about 120 kilometres. There were over 900 dunes to cross, the highest lying towards the northern end. These dunes are not as high as the Simpson's, but the sand is looser. Unlike the Simpson's dunes that run in parallel lines, the Canning's run in all directions, and are known as 'confused' dunes, with many of them having double or more crests which can make driving difficult. We found the track over all the dunes very rough with deep ridges. 'That scalloping of the track is caused by bad driving,' one driver muttered. 'People select the wrong gear to drive over the dune, and half way up they bog and the dune gets chewed up.'

I was rather hoping to photograph some spectacular bogs and see the men use their winches, snatch straps, and other fancy recovery gear that was being carried, but unfortunately they were all such good drivers that the equipment was not needed. Russell's tuition certainly helped — but then there was the threat of the red dunce's cap produced by a fun-loving group of men from Mossvale, who gave it to any driver failing the second attempt to cross a dune. That Russell was the only driver who crossed every dune the first time without stopping, showed very clearly it was indeed a matter of good driving skills.

A big feature of the Canning Stock Route is the wells. Some of them were dry, others had stagnant or brackish water that was suitable only for washing; only about nine wells had good water. Most of the structures of the wells — the windlasses and stock troughs — were in ruins; a few had been burnt out by fires started by lightning strikes. Well 26 had been restored, complete with a stock trough.

One of Russell's co-drivers, Bill Dower, had been one of the few people to drive the full length of the Canning long before the track was well used. In 1974, with three other men, and two vehicles each carrying 125 gallons of petrol (there were no petrol-drops then), they took eighteen days to negotiate it — two of those days being spent bogged in Lake Tobin. Only occasionally did they find a semblance of a track, and driving from well to well they used a compass, sometimes finding it necessary to use a sextant to get more accurate bearings. Bill had brought along his original notes from that trip, and he found that although the structures around many wells had either disintegrated or disappeared, the water in only seven of them had noticeably deteriorated.

Great Oak Forest

Thorny devil

There were many highlights on our trip. From our camp in the Durba Hills, near Well 17, we explored the beautiful Durba Gorge, which contrasted dramatically with the stark, dazzling white expanse of Lake Disappointment, and the stony, yet appealing emptiness of the Gravity Lakes. In the Great Oak Forest lying between Wells 35 and 36, the groves of she-oaks, standing gracefully among the red dunes, whispered in the wind like the murmuring of the sea. Apart from the odd lone camel, we met only one mob of about twenty-five — which was small for this region, as mobs of up to 150 have been sighted. Australia's feral camels, originating from India, are believed to be the only wild camels in the world. Many of the Simpson's camels have been rounded up, as access to that desert is relatively easy, but those in the Great Sandy Desert have been left alone because of its remoteness.

On the whole we saw very few living creatures. Some galahs hung around Well 40, and at Well 41 masses of finches flew in when we drew some water into the old stock trough. Someone had an encounter with a snake in the camp at Well 30, but there was no chance of identifying it because the poor creature was dead and buried within seconds of being sighted; nobody in our group seemed very interested in snakes. It was a different story with another reptile we met: the enchanting little thorny devil that inhabits the deserts of central and Western Australia. So many people wanted to photograph the lizard that he didn't know which way to turn. Growing to about 20 centimetres in length, this rather grotesque-looking creature is quite harmless, and lives entirely on a diet of black ants.

By the time we reached Well 51, the last well on the Canning Stock Route, the temperature had climbed to near 35°C. Before tasting civilisation again, there was one important place to see: the Wolf Creek meteorite crater. Lying at the far north-western edge of the Tanami Desert and 146 kilometres from Halls Creek, this great crater measuring 850 metres in diameter and 50 metres deep, is the second largest in the world (the biggest one is in the United States). Technically speaking, it is believed to be the largest one with the most unbroken rim — others are inclined to be very uneven. It all depends on the way the asteroid hits the ground: if it comes in at an angle, the crater will be more irregular than if it comes straight down — as it did at Wolf Creek.

I had already seen the crater from the air, and had suspected it would be visually more interesting from above than from the ground. I was wrong: it was just as good viewing it from the top of its rim. A ten minute walk from the top led to the intriguing small grove of trees growing in its centre. These trees have only appeared in recent times, and one of our group commented there had been considerable growth since his last visit ten years ago.

After a brief stay in Halls Creek, we returned to Alice Springs via the Tanami Track. Running through the Tanami Desert for about 930 kilometres from Billiluna, south of the Wolf Creek Crater to the Stuart Highway near Alice Springs, this route has become a popular access to the Kimberley. It was in excellent condition when we travelled it, though earlier in the year the Western Australian section had been in a very bad state. Fuel is available at Carranya, Rabbit Flat and at the Tilmouth Roadhouse.

The Tanami Desert covers a large area of the Territory north of Alice Springs and west of the Stuart Highway, and pushes into the north-west of Western Australia. It is not as arid as the country's other great deserts. In 1900 gold was found at The Granites, a series of tors lying near the Tanami Track some 500 kilometres from Alice Springs, and a brief rush followed. Interest in the region by large mining companies has persisted for years, and today gold is again being mined. One day the Tanami Track may be even sealed.

Tinsel bush (*Cyanostegia cyanocalyx*), Great Sandy Desert

Wolf Creek meteorite crater

THE DESERTS

Tanami Desert

Great Sandy Desert

Kopperamanna Crossing, Birdsville Track

THE GREAT TRACKS

There are two roads in Australia that over the years have captured the imagination of Australians: an old stock route known as the Birdsville Track; and the original central Australian railway line support road, the Oodnadatta Track. Both are historic routes.

The Birdsville Track used to be one of the most important — and notorious — of the stock routes in Australia when drovers overlanded cattle to properties, or markets. In the days of early settlement roads were non-existent, and only the great stock routes linked the outback with the rest of the world. Running for some 500 kilometres from Birdsville in south-east Queensland to Marree in South Australia, the Birdsville Track opened when the Port Augusta–Oodnadatta railway was built in the 1880s. From the rich cattle country of south-west Queensland, many minor routes converged on the small town of Birdsville, where the cattle were assembled into great mobs of up to 10 000 head, and then driven south to the railhead at Marree.

Sometimes the Track provided easy travelling; at other times, it was so grim that someone once said it would break the heart of an archangel. In wet years the floods stretched for many kilometres, and in the dry times, sand and dust storms periodically swept the country with a red, stinging ferocity. Over the years several large mobs of cattle perished on this route. Only the artesian bores established by the South Australian government made it possible for stockmen — and mailmen — to travel it during drought. The area is supposed to get an annual rainfall of 100 mm, but when big rains come, that amount may be trebled. In summer, temperatures may soar to over 45°C.

The cattle no longer have to walk the routes, but are taken south by road transport. The Birdsville Track was upgraded in the early 1970s and has become a popular road for tourists travelling to far north-west Queensland. However, even today, it must not be taken lightly as death has always stalked the Track. Even since it was upgraded, quite a few lives have been lost when travellers either ran out of petrol and water, or had mechanical breakdowns during the summer months. Many who died left their vehicles to seek help, and in doing so, they broke a cardinal rule of the outback: stay by your vehicle in the event of breakdown.

The Birdsville Track skirts some of the driest areas in Australia, with the Simpson Desert to the west, and Sturt's Stony Desert to the east; both encroach on it in places. The land is flat, with claypans and great seas of glittering red gibbers that stretch to distant horizons, shimmering with mirages; then sand-dunes roll on and on, sometimes giving way to roughly hewn hills of quartzite rock, in the form of mesas and buttes. The only trees are those by the occasional dry creek bed and around old ruins.

The ruins stand as memorials to vanquished hopes. Like elsewhere in the outback, in the years of good rains the early pioneers went out eagerly to settle, built homes and brought their families; but many overstocked the land, years passed without rain, and in the fight for survival the land usually won. Only the largest stations managed to survive. Today there are some along the Track; the largest is Clifton Hills, of about 28 500 square kilometres. The only petrol for sale is at Mungerannie Station's roadhouse, opened in 1986.

Like the cattle drives of old, a motoring journey along the Birdsville Track — now mostly a wide earth highway — can be easy, or it can be difficult: it all depends on the grader and the weather. If the grader has recently been over it — particularly on the rougher northern end around Goyders Lagoon — and the weather is cool and stable, it is a pleasant trip and can be made in a suitable 2WD vehicle. However, because the Track isn't graded very regularly, it is not recommended for the average 2WD family car; indeed, considerable damage could be done to the car, especially its tyres. It takes little rain to turn it into a strictly 4WD route. When the rain has stopped, if the road is chewed up by vehicles travelling on the soft surfaces before they have had a chance to dry out, then it can be an extremely rough drive for all vehicles.

A Highways Department supervisor I met on the Track explained what happens to the road after rain: 'The heavier the vehicle, the deeper will be the wheel ruts. And if they bog, which they often do, it's worse. Then the sun comes out and dries the muddy ruts iron-hard and the travellers make detours to avoid the original road. After the next lot of rain more detours are made around the old ones, and so it goes on, and the road becomes one hell of a mess. If we haven't been able to get our graders in to do something about it, the length of the road has increased considerably from the figure stated on the signposts and maps.'

These days the Highways Department is usually quick to close the Track after heavy rain, which is good because it can be a nightmare when it is very wet. Some years ago, after an exceptionally wet winter, I travelled it with a party of three 4WD vehicles, and the boggy stretches were so bad that one day we only managed 70 kilometres. When we reached Goyders Lagoon on the last leg of the trip it was dark, and the Track lay under shallow water for quite a few kilometres. Then, about halfway through the stretch of water, one of the vehicles had a flat tyre. It took far more time to get the barbecue plate out from the bottom of all the gear in the vehicle (it was needed to put under the jack in the mud) than it did to change the tyre. I remember arriving at the Birdsville pub at 1.30 a.m., everyone tired and hungry, and receiving a marvellously warm welcome from the publican and his wife — but that was typical of Birdsville.

The Birdsville Hotel, built in 1884, is one of the great pubs of the outback — not in size, but in character. The town's population is around 85, but for one week in September the place hums with up to 6000 people who come from all over the country for the annual Birdsville Races — probably the most famous race meeting in Australia after the Melbourne Cup. It has been held every year since 1882 and is a two-day event. Once, I was in the town a few days before the big week. The pub was certainly ready for the event, and the publican showed me some of his stock that would slake the thirsts of the crowd. He opened the door to the room by the bar, and at the entrance stood a wall of beer cans: the entire room was packed to the ceiling with beer. 'That room will be empty in four days,' he said.

Bogged on the Birdsville Track

Birdsville hotel

Gibber plain, Birdsville Track

Spring wildflowers by Cooper Creek, near Etadunna

My happiest times on the Birdsville Track have been when the normally dry Cooper Creek floods over the road at Kopperamanna Crossing, 144 kilometres north of Marree. It is supposed to happen only about every fourteen to twenty years, but occasionally may occur more often: it all depends on the rains in eastern Queensland as they cause the Cooper to flow — not rain falling in South Australia. Sometimes the flooded Cooper reaches Lake Eyre. When the Birdsville Track is cut by the Cooper, a punt carries traffic across its narrowest section of about 400 metres, east of Etadunna. Downstream at Kopperamanna the water may stretch for about six kilometres and, some distance upstream, at the peak of the flood, it can spread up to 130 kilometres over the plains.

It is the camping along the banks of the Cooper that I enjoy so much. The first time I saw it in flood was in 1974, when it was running at the highest level in recorded history. With a friend, I spent a magical week exploring the Cooper — and eating piles of fish that the two men operating the punt had caught. They seemed grateful for our company, and even took us out in their boat. We learnt a lot about the life of a Cooper Creek puntman. 'At least you have a mate to work with here,' said one of the men. 'Some jobs in the outback can be very lonely. I always reckon it's time to clear out when you put your hat on a post and start talking to it — worse if you argue with it.'

There seemed little chance of that happening to them here. Life was pretty good for these blokes. When they weren't fishing they shot rabbits and ducks, and when it got too hot for sporting pastimes there was always a cold beer to drink and westerns to read. In those days there wasn't much traffic — or even other campers. The puntmen thought it was a busy day when eight vehicles passed through. It was a different story in 1990 when I last saw the Cooper in flood: the punt carried around 100 vehicles a day during the winter tourist season; and someone was even running commercial boat tours. Those puntmen had no time even to think about putting their hats on a post for a conversation.

The Oodnadatta Track also starts at Marree, and runs for 620 kilometres in a north-westerly direction, joining the Stuart Highway at Marla. From Marree to Oodnadatta the road mostly follows the old central Australian railway line, which was re-located to an all-weather route farther west in 1980. The railway first came to Oodnadatta in 1911, and until the line reached Alice Springs in 1929, the town was a chief supply point for the Centre and had a large Afghan camel caravan depot. From here teams of camels, each caravan with up to 80 camels and sometimes driven by only one Afghan, over-landed goods to settlements further north. The train that eventually replaced these cara-vans was named 'The Ghan', after the Afghan cameleers; the modern train on the replaced line retains that name.

Until 1980 there was a string of fettlers' camps by the railway line and the Oodnadatta Track was a very rough road that after rain turned into even more of a quagmire than the Birdsville Track. Today, it has been upgraded and even re-routed in some spots and, when dry, it is generally easier to travel than the Birdsville Track. Many of the fettlers' old stone cottages have become historical points of interest, and some are being restored; there are even plans to turn some into small tourist resorts, complete with camping grounds, walking trails and camel rides. Some people may grumble at this commercialism for the Oodnadatta Track, but unless somebody is willing to restore the old buildings, they will fall victim to vandals who have already wrecked many of them.

Old fettlers' camp, Beresford, Oodnadatta Track

Once the camel caravans were no longer required, and the railway line eventually re-routed, Oodnadatta shrank to a small-sized settlement. A growing number of tourists now pass through, and although there isn't much to see here, the place has character. Nobody could miss the service station: the entire building has been painted a near-fluorescent pink, appropriately called 'The Pink Roadhouse'.

For those people who remember the days when the trains ran through the town, it is a pleasant trip down memory-lane to visit the historic railway station and its museum. Who could ever forget a journey on the old Ghan? The narrow gauge line only permitted the train to travel at a maximum speed of 40 kilometres per hour, mostly it averaged 18; this gave the passengers plenty of time to examine thoroughly every stone, dune, bush and telegraph pole — and the wedge-tailed eagles that occasionally topped them. Sometimes it was necessary to stop the train so the engine driver could throw sand on the lines to get more traction on the slight slopes. After rain, sometimes it took a week to reach Alice Springs, instead of the usual two days.

The Ghan was so famed for its slow travel that a story goes that at one of the many halts a passenger asked the guard why they had stopped. He was told there was a cow on the line. Twenty minutes later there was another halt, and the passenger said to the guard, 'I suppose you are going to tell me there's another cow on the line.' The guard replied, 'That's right — except it's the same cow. It followed us up the line.'

Oodnadatta is also the centre of a huge pastoral area — one of the cattle stations, Anna Creek, is the largest in the world, covering over 30 000 square kilometres. Much of the country along the Track is gibber plain, which gave rise to the saying that the devil made Oodnadatta and was so dissatisfied that he threw stones at it. Petrol is also available on the Track at William Creek, 204 kilometres north of Marree. A tourist brochure magnanimously described William Creek as one of the smallest towns in South Australia: the 'town' is a small pub, a couple of petrol bowsers, and a public telephone box.

Historical interest aside, the Oodnadatta Track provides access to some of the unique mound springs, the series of artesian springs that occur from Dalhousie at the south-western edge of the Simpson Desert to near Marree. They lie at the southern rim of the Great Artesian Basin, and are fed by the basin's underground flow of water. As their name suggests, they are mounds of earth with springs of water at the top, formed by drifting sands and the action of artesian springs, which deposit heavy mineral salts as the water evaporates. As the mounds built up over time, water collected at the top, spilling over the side in one or more places before it eventually dried up.

The size of the mounds varies greatly; some of the extinct ones rise to about 40 metres from the plain, others are only a few metres high. The largest pools are at Dalhousie, now in the Witjira National Park, lying north of Oodnadatta. Spring Hut Pool has become a Mecca for 4WD enthusiasts, who spend days camped by the idyllically warm pool: at the water's edge the temperature is around 34°C, but out in the middle it is noticeably warmer in the spots where bubbles stream energetically to the surface. Many mounds at Dalhousie are topped with impenetrable forests of date palms, giving them an oasis-like appearance on the surrounding desolate plains.

Ruins, Strangways, Oodnadatta Track

Old fettlers' camp, Warrina, Oodnadatta Track

THE GREAT TRACKS

The classic mound spring is Blanche Cup, lying seven kilometres from Coward Springs on the Oodnadatta Track. Resembling a miniature volcano, it rises about ten metres above the plain and is topped by a lovely circular pool edged with grasses. Like many of these thermal springs it appears to be gradually drying up — probably because of the massive siphoning-off of artesian water through bores during this century. I first visited Blanche Cup in 1974, when it was more active than it is now. Then, at irregular intervals, masses of tiny bubbles rose to the surface, and the pool looked like a pot of water just starting to simmer. On a visit in 1990, I found the pool to be smaller with sedges spreading thickly into it, and there was no sign of any bubbling.

I may have been saddened to see changes in Blanche Cup, but the other active spring in the area, the Bubbler, showed no sign of becoming extinct; indeed, this delightful entertainer was bigger and performed better in 1990 than it did in '74. The Bubbler's water churned about every ten minutes or so and a growing bubble of mud struggled to escape. Sometimes it burst with great aplomb, but at other times it just disappeared

Curdimurka, Oodnadatta Track

slowly. I discovered about once in every 90 minutes or so the water swirled even more frantically than usual, and produced an enormous bubble that almost covered the pool. But it was not easy watching the Bubbler on that visit: a gale raged over the plains, and just as the pool formed its biggest bubble of the day, a very strong gust blew the camera and tripod on to the ground.

The Bubbler may still be performing, but not as it did many decades ago: locals say that the bubble used to shoot about a metre into the air. During a visit to the area in the 1980s, I thought the Bubbler had all but dried up, but in fact I mistook the spring known as the Little Bubbler for the big one. When I thrust my hand into the Little Bubbler's warm mud the sensation was similar to that of a gentle massage. Today, it is easy to find both Blanche Cup and the Bubbler as they are fenced off, to protect them from wandering stock. However, when driving around this area, it is important to stick to the main tracks, as the place is one giant claypan. After only a small amount of rain the ground is treacherous for vehicles — even for 4WDs.

Blanche Cup mound spring

Spring Hut Pool, Dalhousie

The Bubbler, near Coward Springs

THE GREAT TRACKS

Sunset, Killalpaninna, near the Birdsville Track

THE GREAT TRACKS

Walls of Wilpena Pound at sunrise

FLINDERS RANGES

The Flinders Ranges in South Australia are one of the best-loved areas in the country, and most people need little excuse to see them. Visitors come in their thousands, many returning to favourite camping sites every year. There is a special atmosphere here, which is almost emotive, in the profusion of magnificent river red gums that line creeks and roads with backdrops of softly rounded hills and higher rugged ranges. If the winter rains have been good, then carpets of red wild hops and purple salvation jane add brilliant colour to some of the scenes. At dawn and dusk the ranges are glorious. Artists and photographers are particularly sensitive to this beauty — I invariably find that I use more film here than elsewhere in Australia, except possibly in the Kimberley.

The Flinders extend for nearly 400 kilometres from around Crystal Brook, north of Adelaide, to just south of Lake Eyre. However, it is the region north of Hawker that is generally considered part of the outback. As Hawker is only a few hours' drive from Adelaide, and less than two days from Melbourne, this is the closest outback country to the densely populated south-eastern portion of Australia.

Excellent bitumen roads link the ranges with civilisation. The road to Wilpena Pound, a major scenic attraction, is sealed, and on the western side, the bitumen has reached Lyndhurst. There are no 'horror stretches' along main routes: many of the gravel roads are maintained regularly, and quite a few of the tracks winding through the gorges and other scenic drives are suitable for 2WD vehicles providing there has been no recent rain. It is not unusual for months to pass without rain falling here, but when it does come, flash flooding is common. Once off the main tourist roads, a 4WD vehicle is usually needed.

One of the finest landforms in the Flinders Ranges, and certainly the best known is Wilpena Pound. Situated 53 kilometres north of Hawker, this large rock basin surrounded with outward-facing cliffs measures eleven kilometres in length and nearly five kilometres across its middle portion; from the air it resembles a huge mountainous dish. The only access into it is via a gap through which Wilpena Creek flows. The nineteenth-century settlers named this natural amphitheatre a 'pound' because it resembled a stock enclosure; the Aboriginal name, Wilpena, means 'the place of bent fingers'.

From the middle of last century to 1920, Wilpena Pound was under lease first to pastoralists, then to wheat farmers, who abandoned it in 1914 after an exceptionally heavy flood swept away their main access road. Today the Pound is part of the Flinders Ranges National Park. The old homestead, a small brick building, still stands among the collection of stately gums at the Pound's entrance, a memorial to the early pioneering days of the district.

Bunyeroo Valley, summer

Old river gum, Prices Creek

Brachina Gorge

Moralana Scenic Drive

There are some very good walking tracks in and around the Pound, all developed by the Adelaide Bushwalking Club, and now maintained by the park rangers. As in the rest of the ranges, walking can be physically demanding, especially in hot weather, since many tracks pass over some extremely rough, waterless ground. One popular hike is to the highest point, St Mary's Peak, rising 1170 metres over the encircling ranges. From the chalet and camping ground set near the Pound's entrance, it is a six- to seven-hour circuit. A shorter walk, to Wangara Lookout on the hill just behind the old homestead, takes about three-quarters of an hour. One summer afternoon I found the views from here particularly arresting: the distant jagged walls, now veiled in soft mauve shadows, gave way to verdant woodland of native pines and gums; between the clumps of trees the cleared grassy areas gleamed fields of pale gold, giving the impression that wheat crops grew there once again.

Summer is not the most popular time to visit the Flinders. Normally I go in spring, but once, for a change, I decided to see it in summer. Although the mid-north of the State can be very hot at that time, this proposed trip was not as crazy as it seemed; I reasoned it need not be too much of an ordeal providing a few precautions were taken. I was well rewarded for the effort, because the beauty and distinctive atmosphere of the Flinders — particularly around the Wilpena Pound area — was more exhilarating than in the spring. Somehow the summer scenes were essentially more Australian.

That January I was acutely aware of richer colours: the warm browns of the earth and the brilliant yellows of sun-ripened grass glowed against the green of the native pines and the shadowy blues and purples, fiery reds and delicate pinks of the ranges. Even the beauty of the river gums was accentuated by the vibrant summer hues. To top it off, the warmth released many delectable tangy scents from the earth and vegetation. As for the birds, the raucous cries of cockatoos, galahs and corellas as they restlessly flew from tree to tree, seemed even more an integral part of the scene than in the cooler months.

My base was Wilpena Pound. Not only was it cooler there because of the higher altitude, but the shop at the camping ground provided one vital commodity: ice. The temperature hovered mostly around 35°C, but one ghastly day it rose to 43°C. If I were to do it again, I would stay at Wilpena's motel — camping in temperatures over 40°C without a nearby waterhole to dip into is my idea of hell. The nights were pleasant, but the early mornings were superb — and that was when I ran around taking photos. By nine o'clock it was time to find a shady spot and stay parked until just after sunset.

Apart from the beautiful scenery, that summer I was aware of other little things; for instance, in many places the ants were much more active than in the cooler months. At times I had trouble setting up the camera in the spot I wanted because the little pests kept running up my legs and the tripod's. But it was the bees that gave cause for sorrow. There weren't many around, but whenever I put a bowl of water outside the campervan, about half a dozen would hover thirstily over the water, then attempt to drink from the steep sides. Inevitably they fell in and drowned. Then one of them discovered a small pool of spilt water on the table, and in fascination I watched as it drank carefully from the pool's edge.

Just about every road in the Flinders could be called a 'scenic drive'. I have many favourites, but the one I return to again and again is the Moralana Scenic Drive, linking the Leigh Creek Road in the west and the Wilpena–Hawker Road in the east. This lovely route runs for 28 kilometres, passing the superbly contoured Elder Range and the majestic south-western walls of Wilpena Pound. In spring, if it is a good season for flowers, many slopes are covered with salvation jane. For much of the way the track stays close to Moralana Creek and its forest of river gums, their stout, mottled silver-grey trunks giving such character to the landscape. Towards the eastern end, native pines grace the slopes — not thickly, but spread out to give the effect of parkland. I like to make this trip from both directions — from east to west, and from west to east, preferably early morning or late afternoon.

Another favourite drive in spring is the loop road from Blinman to Parachilna, via Glass Gorge: in a good year I have seen the hills near the Parachilna end dyed a brilliant red with wild hops. On this road you get the best views of the scenery by travelling from east to west; but in taking this loop drive, you shouldn't miss seeing the scenery along the more direct route to Blinman from Parachilna Gorge. Parts of the Glass Gorge track are rough, so take care if you have a 2WD vehicle.

Elder Range

FLINDERS RANGES

Then there is the fantastic drive from Wilpena to Brachina Gorge, via the Aroona Valley and returning through Bunyeroo Gorge. Both places are worth seeing; indeed, a traveller passing through earlier this century declared the country between Wilpena and Aroona 'to be the loveliest in Australia'. I cannot visit Brachina without staying overnight: it's that sort of place, particularly in a good spring when salvation jane splashes colour through the gorge. Running for several kilometres, this long gorge is guarded by massive craggy walls that tower dramatically over the track and creek. After heavy rain, this is no place for 2WD vehicles — or at times even for 4WDs — because in places the track runs through the normally low creek that after rain may turn into a raging flood. Having once been trapped in Brachina with very little food, I always carry extra provisions whenever I camp in any of the gorges in case the creeks rise and prevent me getting out. My experience has been that in a good year for wild-flowers, the winter rains responsible for the growth of the flowers often continue into the spring.

The ranges become wilder and more stark as they march northwards. In the Arka-roola–Mount Painter Sanctuary, the country is noted for its untamed, rugged mountains edged with razor-like ridges plummeting to rocky valleys below, and for the narrow spurs and saddles that offer stunning vistas of tier after tier of folded stony slopes, even-tually giving way to the vast northern plains. The area, with its wealth of minerals, has long been a paradise for rockhounds. For the keen botanist, a good spring season will provide more diversity of species than in any other part of the Flinders.

A good road runs to the Arkaroola–Mount Painter Sanctuary, and the drive from the south via Copley is particularly scenic. Now that the roads have been improved in the east Flinders, many people return via Wertaloona and Wirrealpa to see Chambers Gorge, an impressive eighteen-kilometre cleft running through the range towards Lake Frome. In the Arkaroola–Mount Painter Sanctuary, Arkaroola Village offers a wide range of facilities, including motel accommodation and a camping ground. There is also an astronomical observatory containing a very good telescope through which visitors can observe the heavens, and learn something about astronomy from Doug Sprigg, who runs it. Arkaroola's clear, dark skies are ideal for seeing the stars.

The village is 550 metres above sea level, and consequently has a pleasant climate — certainly it is cooler here in summer than it is in the lower areas. There are many delightful gorges and beautiful waterholes to explore by car and on foot, and some of the places have equally delightful names: Nooldoonooldoona, Bolla Bollana, Barrarranna, Sitting Bull and Dinnertime Hill.

The highlight at Arkaroola is the Ridgetops Tour, said to be one of the most thrilling scenic drives in Australia. For safety reasons, the tortuous 30 kilometres that run along the mountain ridges is closed to the public, so it is necessary to take a tour from the village. However, for 4WD enthusiasts, other back roads open to the public give splen-did views over the ridgetops.

I always enjoy the village's Ridgetop Tour. On my last visit, in October, I had hoped to take one at dawn, but as the mornings were still pretty cold, nobody was very enthu-siastic; instead, I went on the afternoon trip. When we reached the incredible spur at Sillers Lookout, shadows were starting to fill the valleys, allowing the folds in the ranges to stand out boldly in relief. On the way back, the distinct peak of Mount Painter blushed a warm pink in the setting sun. I couldn't help thinking that the Ridgetops Tour was a most suitable climax to a visit to the Flinders Ranges.

Parachilna Gorge

Sturt Desert Pea (*Clianthus formosus*)

Corellas

Freeling Heights, Arkaroola

Sillers Lookout, Arkaroola ridgetops

Dune, south-west New South Wales

BEYOND THE BLACK STUMP

The black stump is anywhere in the outback. Celebrated in Australian folklore, it is the proverbial outward limit of civilisation, or a place lying at the edge of a mythical horizon; it may even be a gateway to the outback. Whatever the definition, it conjures up in the mind's eye 'remoteness'. This colloquialism is used in expressions referring to some thing or place being 'this side of the black stump' or 'beyond the black stump'.

Its origins are as vague as the black stump itself, but a blackened stump of some kind was undoubtedly a frequent bush landmark for early country dwellers, and it often became a local place name. Many districts in Queensland, New South Wales and Victoria claim the original 'black stump' because their early records have listed Black Stump creeks, tanks, swamps, resting places and even a wine saloon. New South Wales' Coolah probably has the soundest claim, as in 1826 Governor Darling proclaimed the limit of the area in which settlement might be allowed in the new colony: the Black Stump sheep run at Coolah was named a boundary. However, motorists passing through Blackall on Queensland's Landsborough Highway are left in no doubt that it originated here: a big sign at the entrance to the town advises that Blackall is the 'home of the fair-dinkum black stump'.

Everyone has a different black stump. For me, it lies in various places. I think of the seemingly endless wide plains lying beyond any of the outback's towns. Some people say these plains are boring and scream of dullness, but I find mental relaxation and freedom in their emptiness and refreshing simplicity. Once, while I was travelling over the Barkly Highway, I was suddenly aware that the landscape contained only three features: the grey ribbon of bitumen, an unbroken expanse of bright yellow grass, and a blue sky lacking any clouds. No tree, bush, rock, or pole graced the scene. But, true to the ever-changing nature of the outback's plains, it soon changed. As I watched the trees and shrubs beginning to appear again, I felt almost as if they were intruders; even more of an intrusion was a building, even though it appeared ant-sized under the spaciousness of the land and sky.

I think of the plains in far western New South Wales. Out from Broken Hill, the low, stony ranges give way to vast areas dotted with saltbush, spindly grasses, pebbles and the odd sand-dune. Here, between Bourke and Wentworth the mighty Darling River twists its way like a writhing snake for some 1000 kilometres before pouring its muddy contents into the Murray River in the far south-west corner of the State. Great river gums line its banks, providing precious shade in an otherwise exposed landscape. The debris from previous floods lying in the water and along its deep banks often gives it an untidy air, yet to my eyes it seems to have a depth of character and beauty unrivalled by any other Australian river.

Salt lake, north of Port Augusta

Wild peas, near Coober Pedy

The Birdsville Track is certainly 'black stump' country. To the west of the Track lie extensive expanses of glittering salt lakes; in one area they are called the Ephemeral Lakes. The greatest of the inland salt lakes is Lake Eyre, where in 1964 Donald Campbell set a land record of 848.6 kilometres per hour in his *Bluebird 2*. Some of the smaller, more intimate saltpans may have more appeal — many are not on the maps, but often Aborigines know them by names others find impossible to pronounce. Could a mere saltpan get the grand name of Noodlawandracooracooratarraninna? This one lies somewhere north-west of Mulka, and apparently it is the Aboriginal name for the kangaroo-rats that breed in the bushes near the saltpan.

If the black stump is anywhere, I think it would have to be in far west Queensland, where many legends have originated. It is here that the uniquely Australian song, 'Once a jolly swagman' was born at Combo Waterhole near Winton. Western Queensland is also home for the Min Min light — the mysterious dancing 'ghost lights' first seen in the 1880s near Boulia, 386 kilometres north of Birdsville, then later elsewhere. Since then, there have been countless sightings, and nowadays at least ten people a year see it.

The Min Min appears at night as a single bright light, like the headlight of an approaching car; one man said it kept pace alongside his vehicle, another said the light split in two just as he was about to run through it. There used to be many sightings as far south as Goyders Lagoon, but now they are mostly confined to a radius of about two hundred kilometres around Boulia. Many people prefer not to report officially any sightings — they don't want to be thought of as cranks. Strangely enough, although most people find an encounter with the light a scary experience, animals are not spooked by it. The Aborigines, who have also seen it, have no explanation — they say it came only after the Europeans arrived. People have tried to chase it, capture it, and even shoot it, all without success. Nobody can explain this strange phenomenon. Although many scientific theories abound (the most popular being it comes from a spontaneous combination of certain gases given off by artesian bores), no explanation satisfies those who have seen this light.

While thinking about the black stump, there is one area that would come to many people's minds: the land around Innamincka, where not so far away a spot is immortalised by a tragic moment in Australian history that is now embedded in the Australian psyche: the Burke and Wills expedition. If anyone went way beyond the black stump, it was Burke and his men. In November 1860 the expedition made its depot camp on the banks of the Cooper. The party split when Burke took Wills, King and Gray with him for the long, hard walk north over unexplored land to the Gulf of Carpentaria, and instructed Brahe to expect them back within three months. If they did not return within that time, he was to wait until his provisions ran low, then take his party back south. After four months with no sign of Burke, Brahe decided to leave.

On that fateful morning of Sunday 21 April, 1861, his party headed south but just before leaving Brahe buried a box of rations in case Burke and his men should return. On a coolibah tree, he carved the instruction DIG 3FT NW, and the date. At 7.30 p.m. on that same day, Burke, Wills and King returned after an appalling journey to the Gulf and back. They dug for the rations and next day staggered onwards, but only King survived and five months later was rescued by Howitt's relief party, which found him living with an Aboriginal tribe.

The 'Dig' tree still grows by the banks of the Cooper, and Burke's grave lies about 25 kilometres away. Today, it is almost a pilgrimage to visit the place. For many Australians, the timeless silence over the land, broken only by the screeching cockatoos in the old gums and coolibahs lining the Cooper, somehow evokes an emotion that goes deeper than patriotism.

Whichever black stump you may be beyond, once night falls, a deep peace falls over the outback. You may even find yourself listening to the silence, it is so profound. And wherever you are, it is easy to marvel at the huge diamond-studded canopy of sky displaying clouds of stars not seen in urban areas, as it presses in close. As you gaze at the flames licking the wood of the companionable campfire, it is also easy to understand how this land eases tensions of people who come from cities that some would say are stress-filled spiritual deserts. This wonderful atmosphere — be it on the banks of the Cooper or elsewhere in Australia's outback — is balm, and inspiration, to the spirit.

Sunrise, Cooper Creek

Darling River

BEYOND THE BLACK STUMP

Walls of China, Lake Mungo, south-west New South Wales

Lake Menindee at sunset, south-east of Broken Hill

Australian pelicans

Outback campfire